SHADOW DANCING

My Journey as My Wife Came Out of the Closet

GARY COOPER

ISBN: 978-1-7979-6781-3

Contents

Chapter 1 1

Chapter 2 7

Chapter 3 13

Chapter 4 17

Chapter 5 19

Chapter 6 21

Chapter 7 23

Chapter 8 29

Chapter 9 33

Chapter 10 35

Chapter 11 41

Chapter 12 49

Chapter 13 55

Chapter 14 63

Chapter 15 71

Chapter 16 77

Chapter 17 83

Chapter 18 85

Chapter 19 99

Chapter 1

I KNEW SOMETHING WAS WRONG the moment I walked into the house. As my feet touched each step on the staircase, I could feel the tightening in the hollow of my chest; something was about to go down.

As I entered the room, Connie turned away quickly, but not quick enough; I had seen what I had seen and it made me uneasy.

First I heard Connie say to someone, "I got to go, bye," hanging up so quickly the phone fell from her hand. If there is one thing you need to know about my ex-wife it is this: she did not rattle easily, and when she did, well, you knew something was wrong.

The next thing that I noticed was her dreamy look that danced across so quickly, like a shadow on the wall. The erotic gleam that so many times was reserved for me seemed to gleam for someone else.

She was practically nude, except for the nightgown that rode up her shapely hips just the way I liked it. One brown nipple peeked out of the top of the gown, which she covered when she saw me looking, licking my dry lips, swallowing deeply. My throat was so dry I had trouble swallowing. To a fault she attempted to hide her obvious aroused state from me.

The weird thing is, for the past month or so, this had been happening a lot. Especially those times when I left the salon and came directly home earlier than usual. Now, it was time to bring this thing—whatever it was—to a head.

"Who was that on the phone?" I asked.

"Nobody," she stammered. "A friend of mine," she added.

"Which is it, nobody or a friend?" I muttered through teeth clenched so tightly I could barely make out what she said. No answer.

I reached down and picked up the phone from the floor and pushed redial. "Hey, baby, did he leave already? Now can we finish. I was about to c—"

"About to what?" I yelled into the phone. "Is that you, Kelly? What's going on here?" Dial tone. She hung up, but I knew.

"So that's it, huh?" I asked. "I can't believe this ..." My voice trailed off as I felt a slump in my stomach. Life as I had known it had just ended.

Over the years I have thought about writing about that day. But I could never bring myself to do so. Of all the painful moments in my life—and there have been a few—none were as painful as this. It would not be an overstatement to say that this was the single most painful time of my life.

Could I force myself to relive all the good and bad memories of one of the darkest relationships of my life?

They say that everything happens for a reason, which means the answer to that question is yes. Hopefully, by writing about what happened I'll understand and may be able to help somebody else who has gone through it to "bounce back" so to speak. Or to help them recognize or pick up on the signs that I didn't see, or saw but didn't understand what I was looking at.

Even still, it was a bittersweet event in my life. On one hand it helped me realize fatherhood, sacrifice, and so much more, but on the other hand made me feel less than a man, scratching my head, wondering what happened. This is not something that happened an hour ago. This took some time. Maybe it was going on before we were married, maybe before we first met. If so, then shouldn't she have told me? And if it didn't start before we were married then it had to have started while we were married. Which is worse?

I thought I was the only one who had gone through something like this, until one day a friend came to me. In an attempt to make me feel better, he told me his story of the same. But then I heard another friend's story, and another, and still another. That's when I realized that rarely does one hear the story of how it affects a man, or what he goes through when confronted with the reality that his wife is in love with another woman.

Her being in love with another man would still have me feeling betrayed, but at least then it would have been a lot easier to understand. It wouldn't have made it right, but losing your wife to a man is a different dynamic. We expect other men to be attracted to our wives, and we expect our wives to see other men they find attractive. But a line has to be drawn, and neither is supposed to cross it.

For me, hearing these stories made it easier for me to say out loud, "MY WIFE HAD COME OUT OF THE CLOSET AS A LESBIAN AND IS IN LOVE WITH ANOTHER WOMAN. There I said it." But then I kept wondering, *Why am I having to say that in the first place?* The sad part is that I'm not the only man who has been confronted with *having* to sort out how to deal with this. And which part do I deal with, her being a lesbian or me being betrayed? And if the answer has to deal with her being a lesbian, does that mean that I'm lesbianhomophobic? And if the answer is my being betrayed, does it mean that I feel betrayed about my wife being a lesbian or that she was sneaking around with someone behind my back? Does it matter that it was a man? Or woman? Do you see where this is going?

But in truth, I don't think that a woman's sexual orientation is the issue because, let's face it, betrayal is betrayal even if you can argue the many reasons that a woman would be afraid to come out. I've heard the many stories of her family disowning her, the stories of being raped by men who believe they can f!#k the lesbian out of her—"She just needs a good one." Or being ostracized from church, when really she, like anyone else, is just there looking for God, and so many other reasons, but that's her journey. In the end it's still betrayal. So the question now is, how do I handle "this" kind of betrayal?

3

Gary Cooper

In a lot of cases, the woman knows that she is a lesbian or that she's attracted to someone of the same sex, coming into the male/female relationship. Or maybe she's "just curious" but conceals it in case that's all it turns out to be for her. But some things are like freckles, and even though you may cover them up, they never go away. And it is hard to keep things that are natural to you inside forever. So for her, freedom became being who she really was. It outweighed anything that she felt for anybody but herself. I would imagine that being who everybody else wanted you to be for most of your life would take its toll on a person, as it did my wife. So the downside sometimes for everybody else is when she finally decides to go down that road, there's very little you can do about it. She takes a whole family and her friends with her whether they want to go or not. And maybe that's her right when it's just her life that will be affected by her decision. But the impact on each family member might not be seen or even noticed right away. It does take a toll. As did ours. And in ways that we never noticed until years later, maybe because you're not dealing with the usual breakup story.(cheating spouse , financial problems , falling out of love etc.).... I'm sure very few breakups happen the way ours did.

There aren't many places to go to see my story. I couldn't turn on the television to some talk show and see a group of men gathered around crying on each other's shoulders, talking about how they felt or how it affected them. Whenever you hear the story of this kind of betrayal talked about on television, if it's about a man coming out, it's always a woman crying and talking about all the things she had to go through when she found out that her husband was gay. But change the story to the woman coming out. Then the discussion turns to, "all she had to go through to hide her deep secret" and "how she finally found the strength and courage to come out." There is never talk about the man, and what he went through; at least I have never seen it. So for me there was nowhere to turn to understand what I was feeling, or if I even had a right to feel what I was feeling

Right now there are a lot of men, a few that I know personally, who have wives or girlfriends who are closet lesbians, and the guys don't even have a clue. Sometimes the signs are staring them right in the face, but they don't know what they're looking at. Like in my case, they probably make excuses and dismiss the signs. Some signs might not seem or look like a sign at all because the thought of something like that to most men is never a thought; that is just how we think.

An example could be your wife exhibiting behavior that if done with a man would make you feel very uncomfortable. Most men would never take a second thought because what's being done is being done with a woman. Sometimes, as men, we only see it as "just girl stuff." That's what we are programmed to believe, so we never see it coming. The thought of our wives looking at a woman the way they would look at a man would never cross our minds. Why it never does is another story. But in time even that will change.

Now this isn't always the way it happens, but for me it did. Reflecting back I think of the night when Lisa, who had become really close friends with my wife, came into the salon that my wife and I owned together. Lisa was a beautiful caramel-complexioned Jamaican woman who commanded a room when she entered. Just the way she carried herself gave off an air of class, and you knew she had to be from a family of prominence there. Her hair, which was once long and silky, was now cut short to reveal her natural wavy hair. And with a body that was well cared for, it was easy to see that she was used to the finer things in life. But Lisa was married to a verbally abusive man, which left her with very little confidence and had her feeling less than the beautiful eye candy that she was.

Now, their marriage had the usual drama that comes with being with an abusive person, like him getting caught with another woman and turning it into an argument to deflect his wrongdoing. He used affection only when trying to make up after his mess up, always criticizing her hair and weight (even though she had a body most women would die for).

Lisa even got into a physical fight with his mother after she came over from Jamaica to stay with them without her prior knowledge and was allowed to disrespect her in her own house.

So the decline of their marriage was like a slow drip that had taken its toll, and by now, they were sleeping in separate bedrooms and, for the most part, living in the same house, passing by each other barely speaking. It became hard for her to live like this. Eventually she left the marriage, later developing a relationship with a woman. A woman, who also had a group of friends.

Most of the women in this circle, at one time, had intimate relationships with men and some of these women also had children and families. All had lives that they walked away from to begin a new life that was more than likely inside them all the time. And even still, some had never been with a man because they knew at an early age their sexual preference. But, most importantly, they all were being who they were. I think that was very liberating for my wife to see. And in time I would come to understand just how this scene had impacted her.

I had no idea that our friendship would be the beginning of my wife's self-discovery. Nor did I know that one sunny Sunday morning, breakfast with my wife and those two friends would drastically change what had started out as a great friendship. Every day was carefree, full of excitement. But my life was about to take one hell of a turn! I was about to learn, firsthand, how hard it would be to handle my wife coming out of the closet.

Chapter 2

MY LIFE STARTED OUT LIKE any other black male growing up in the fifties and sixties. Being a part of segregation and integration, it was those communities that shaped my view of what a man or woman should be like, or better yet, what a family should look like. Boys ran, climbed trees, played marbles, etc. And even when it came to the opposite sex, boys got a pat on the head from their fathers for having "all those girls calling the house"; however, that didn't apply to the girls. They were taught how to cook, clean, do laundry, and save themselves for their husbands. Even then, there must have been a gay and lesbian community around me somewhere. But because of the time, it was so well hidden that we never saw even a hint of it. Even so, we never gave it much thought. The girls around us who played just as hard as any one of us boys, we just saw as being a "tomboy." Or another childhood friend who was a boy but preferred to play dolls with the girls also was just a "sissy." We never looked at them as either as gay or lesbian because we had never even heard the word *lesbian*, and the word *gay* meant to be happy. They were just friends we played with. That was just how things were in those days.

As we became teenagers and started high school, that same girl left her tomboy ways and became this drop-dead gorgeous girl with all the trimmings, which made us all see her in a whole different light and wonder, *Where was this girl when we were growing up?* That little boy who played with the girls and dolls graduated with us, joined, and retired from the Marines. Now this says nothing about their sexuality. But neither turned out the way their early days suggested they would turn out. Or maybe they did, but to us it never mattered; they were just

7

our friends from the hood. We all graduated from high school and went out into the world to experience the world beyond our little community. Hey, we had no idea

I was a musician and went through most of my early years having more interest in music than girlfriends. I never had a chance to get too involved in a close, meaningful relationship. Sometimes I didn't end relationships in the best way possible. But in my youth and immaturity, I didn't see a better way. Or maybe since my music was more important, I didn't desire to see a better way, meaning I hadn't figured out where women and relationships fit into my life yet. Most came in competing with my love for music, and since that was my mind-set at the time, it's safe to say I made the worst boyfriend. Most of my relationships were very secondary, and I'm sure most of the women thought I lacked the capacity to feel and express love. But the reality is I think, like most musicians or band boys, in the early years we tend to have a problem making the connection between love of music and love of women. I think we are willing to go a further distance for our music than we are willing to go for our women. I think for us, we didn't understand the balance of nurturing both and them occupying the same space at the same time.

I think people of the arts, such as actors, musicians, artists, and other occupations in the entertainment business, mostly have that attitude. I think that's why we tend to go through so many relationships. For us, we are willing to go wherever we have to go or do to break out our craft. I think this is where love, business, music, and reality collide. And this is what made me willing to go wherever I needed to go for music but not love. That was the difference between Connie and any other relationship. I had found a partner.

But before I got to that point, I guess I had to go through the whole music business rise and fall experience to have a story to tell, and music took me all over the country trying to get to that place.

I met many people during my music journey, some good, some bad, some ruthless, and some just like me, just looking for an outlet and trying to figure it out. All I knew was that music was my passion, which meant most of my early days were spent trying to break into the record industry. By 1979, my group and I had landed a recording contract with a major record label that produced a Top 20 records. By this time, I was willing to do almost anything to get to the next level, like move to New York, Atlanta, or wherever I thought was a good place to live with a Top 20 record.

Without going through the whole story of life for us when we were in the business, the breaking point for me came sometime around the mid-80s when I one day had a complete meltdown. I became tired of my group's manager screwing us one last time. I got so fed up with him one day that I left my apartment on West 78th and Columbus on my way to East 93rd and 1st Ave. I don't have a very intimidating look and have always been able to hail a cab. But on this day I couldn't. I started walking, cutting through Central Park. While walking, I had actually rationalized killing my manager and getting ten years but doing only six years for good behavior. Not a great career move, but at the time, it made sense.

When I got to 6th, the street was blocked due to a movie shoot. So I had to walk several blocks more to get around it. By that time, it was like I had just run for fifty miles. I was trying to suck in as much air as I could to catch my breath. I stopped and realized that I had taken this far too seriously. I think my state of mind was: working very hard, making the right decisions about which label to sign with, countless hours in the studio, many sacrifices. And to have one person come along and jeopardize all that work, well, somebody had to die. So in my negative state of mind, I was starting to make the most destructive behavior seem rational. That's where I was heading. That's when I realized New York was not where I needed to be.

Gary Cooper

I left New York for Atlanta. I realized it would have been the same there for me. Then I went back to Florida where I floated around trying to find my place in life. I ran into a good friend, Tammy Francis. Tammy was an interior decorator who had designed a new club called "Tease." She also was part owner, along with her husband and four other partners. Since I had experience playing clubs, she invited me to run one. I started by doing the books and came to the conclusion that no matter how packed the club was, it could never make a profit because the overhead was way too high. To my surprise that didn't matter to them. I think their pride in their image of being the local black movers and shakers wouldn't let them close it. So I figured, *Okay, I have to figure out how to make it work.* The concern was to keep it packed, so I had a sound system built, a lighting system, fog machine, New York DJ, and a new attitude that brought in the people. I hired my company, Cooper and Associates Marketing and Advertising to handle promotions.

Soon we were bringing in recording groups to do shows. The people were coming in good numbers. One in particular was an old friend, Judy, who was with her cousin, Connie. We were introduced but really didn't talk much. Most of my attention was on Judy, so much so, that Connie thought we had something going on. But throughout the night, our eyes would catch one another's. I thought she was a sexy woman the way she wore her hair straight, and flowing, with one side tucked behind her ear and the other side pulled down over one eye. She had a kind of a mysterious vibe about her, and at some point she approached me about doing a Mother's Day fashion show at the club. So began our first one-on-one talk. Even though it was related to business, we still connected somehow. I guess you can say our conversation was more of a mixture of business, with a little nightclub flirting mixed in.

In putting together the Mother's Day fashion show we spent many hours together. She had specific ideas about how she wanted the stage to look, the posters to look, the tickets, the color, the music throughout the night, the food menu, and even the sound of the radio commercials. I just had to make it all happen, and I did.

The Mother's Day show was a success. But I was glad it was over. At the same time I was talking with my old band mates about starting the group back. But after the experience of doing the show with Connie, I saw that it wasn't that I had to be in a group; I just needed an artistic outlet. To be involved in something where I could be creative is what I found in advertising and promotions.

We started looking for the next show to do and realized there were many projects that could be put together by our two companies that would give us both outlets to bring about what was missing in both of our lives.

When I met Connie, I didn't know that I would soon care for her so much that she would become more important to me than music. Even when I met her I was trying to get out of a relationship with someone who was holding suicide over my head. I guess looking back and being young and dumb, the threat of suicide seemed like a good reason to stay in a relationship. I mean, who wants to be the reason that someone killed himself or herself? But at some point I realized that it was a game and called her bluff, by saying to her, "Look, this relationship is not working out, so I am done," and waited to see if anything would happen. Of course, I could have been wrong but nothing happened. Once I got through that drama, I was able to breathe again and focus on one woman.

That is when I realized that this was the woman who I wanted to spend the rest of my life with. And even though we came from two different countries, culturally we were still in the same place.

Connie came from Jamaica at age thirteen where she and her two sisters lived with their father. They came to America to live with their mother. It was the typical island upbringing—cook, clean, get a good education, work hard, save your money, show very little emotion, and make sure you don't have to depend on a man.

I think my coming from an affectionate family that said, "I love you" and showed it was a balance to her upbringing, which was more like, "I must love you because I'm taking care of you aren't I?" Our balance made our relationship grow, even in business.

But Connie looked the opposite of one's perception of what a lesbian is supposed to look like, and with her back ground in modeling, she knew how to put together clothes and make them look chic. She was 5'6" or 5'7", slender with long slightly bowed legs, straight hair parted over to one side, and she always dressed in black. It gave a bit of mystery to her image.

Having been married twice before, Connie seemed cautious about letting anyone too deep inside her heart. I had never been married. Never gave it any thought. And to be honest up until these days, I always thought I would go my whole life single. But through our many long talks, I realized that Connie mostly clubbed and pursued modeling. She had a son named Michael and, from what I could see, didn't play a big part in his early rearing. He had no contact with his biological father. So her families of women were convenient sitters. That gave her plenty of time to pursue modeling. Soon she started a modeling production company. She did shows throughout Miami and Fort Lauderdale and was starting to get a name for herself in the area. She got to use all the ideas from her other shows at our shows.

Chapter 3

THE FIRST INDICATION THAT THINGS were moving in a romantic direction with Connie, even though I didn't realize it at the time, was the night that we sat at her apartment talking. We talked about her life and past relationships, her two failed marriages, and what went wrong, at least by her account. Even though we talked about it at great length, the missing pieces to the puzzle would not be put in place until years later. All these failed marriages were interconnected. All I knew is that we had so much in common, and I had lost track of the time. I got up and went to the window to look out and, to my amazement, I saw daylight. We had talked all night without realizing it.

I had to get home. My mom was with my son, Jermaine, who I was raising at the time . But I also had 4 boys , Maurice, Cory, Marcus, and Koron . Also 1 daughter Joy that lived with their Moms. So I had to get home. As I left I told her good-bye. She responded by saying, "I love you." The look on her face showed that she was just as surprised as I was. We both hugged and I left. All the way home I kept replaying that scene in my mind over and over again. Soon we became attached at the hip. The next move was obvious: join Cooper and Associates and Simply Connie Productions. She became vice president of my company, and I became vice president of her company.

Simply Connie Productions put on shows and Cooper and Associates did the marketing and advertising. With her experience in modeling and mine in staging concerts, our shows were soon well known throughout South Florida for being sleek and artistic with fog, explosions, moving stage risers, slick choreography, timed music, sharp and unique fashions, and well-thought-out commentating. We also included good spiritual messages in the scenes and themes.

We soon started taking other advertising clients. It became too much. I needed something more stable. The advertising business was starting to feel like the music business—so involved that you have no time for anything else, including family. Connie and I were becoming a couple, and being with her brought out a desire in me to have a family, a real family. I needed to leave home in the morning and come home in the evening. We needed to feel more like a family than a business. We decided to live together.

My son, Jermaine, and I, along with Connie and Michael, moved into an apartment in Plantation, Florida. Immediately we began feeling more like a family. I came along at a time that her son, Michael, needed a father figure in his everyday life. At that time, I also had custody of my own son, Jermaine. Soon they became like brothers. Jermaine didn't take to Connie like Michael had taken to me. So there was always conflict between Connie and Jermaine. But as I see it now, the conflict had more to do with the conflict within herself, which didn't allow her to be that maternal.

My mother, my sister, my aunts, and I nurtured Jermaine. So he was used to being around a different spirit when it came to women. That was more than Connie was capable of giving to her own son, let alone another.

The people who had raised Connie—her mother, her two sisters, her father, and her sister's boyfriends—mostly raised Michael. Connie soon talked about marriage, which meant her saying to me, "I hope you don't think I'm going to be your girlfriend forever." But she was still legally married to her second husband, though separated. We talked about that. I told her that we couldn't get married as long as she was still married to someone else. She soon called my bluff about not being able to marry her because she was already married.

She took the steps to get a divorce, and it was finalized. I remember coming home and seeing this manila envelope in her hands, but she never said what was in it. She kept talking about everything else, the business, her day, and other things but my eyes stayed glued to the envelope. She looked at me and I realized that she was now serious. I looked back at her nervously as she handed me the envelope and said, "Gary, I hope that you're not playing with me." I opened the envelope, spilled the contents, and found they were documents finalizing her divorce. I sat there reading them over and over as if every detail in them mattered the most.

Her marriage was now resolved. I looked at her with the dumb look that men have sometimes when they don't have anything to say. A kind of blank stare. "Okay, I guess we'll have to plan it then." In retrospect, I had no idea what that meant, but that was my response. The rest of the night faded. We started to plan a wedding.

Chapter 4

LIFE TOGETHER TOOK US IN a different direction. Marriage wasn't the only thing on my plate. I was also at another crossroad in my life—what to do about another career. It was time to do something else, something more stable, because our business was starting to feel like the music business. That prayer was answered the night I fell asleep thinking about that question, only to be awakened the next morning by sitting straight up in my bed repeating the question that I was asking when I fell asleep the night before. "Do hair?" I said out loud. It was as if someone had whispered that command in my ear in my sleep. I kept repeating to myself, "Do hair" while looking up at the ceiling like a child questioning his parent. I went back and forth in my mind, because I had never even played in hair let alone styled it.

But at the end of the day, Father knows best. With that, I got the Yellow Pages and turned to beauty schools. My eyes stopped on Hollywood School of Beauty. I called and was greeted on the phone by a girl named Carrie. She told me all about the school and I became interested enough to visit the school the same day. When I got there I was already nervous and looking for a reason to turn around. When I walked into the office there was a line of people. My impatience gave me a good reason to turn around. "Too many people, I'll come back tomorrow." I turned and walked out the door. As I was opening the car door, I heard a voice from behind me call my name, "Gary?" I recognized the voice from the phone.

I turned around and answered, "Yes, I'm Gary." I saw Carrie for the first time. "You're not about to leave are you?" she asked.

"Too many people," I said, "and I have so much to do. I'll come back tomorrow."

She looked at me with a stern motherly look, and said, "If you leave here, you will not come back, because tomorrow will bring about another excuse. Come with me, I'll take you back in with me and get you signed up." She took my hand and led me past the line and to her office. That's how I got started in the hair business.

After about three months, I suggested to Connie that she should enroll too. We could become a hairstyling couple. "I'll start next year," was her reply.

"No, you need to start now," I said, "because next year will turn into the next year, then the next and by then this window will be closed." After a few days she enrolled. We attended the same school at different shifts to make it easier for work and family life. That period of going to school had its own stories, but that's another book.

We soon finished school and got our cosmetology licenses. The next task was to find jobs as hairstylists. At that time, it was easier for males to find hairstylist jobs in the salons than for women, so I had an easier time of it than Connie. It was our intention to work as a styling team, so when I found a job I convinced the owner to hire Connie too.

Once again, we were working side by side and marriage felt like the next sensible step. And yet, before that came about, we took a detour spiritually into African culture.

Chapter 5

DURING THE ORGANIZING OF OUR wedding, we were introduced to Chief Ajamu who would later perform our ceremony. It was he who helped us understand that an African wedding had more to do with the ceremony than the clothes you were wearing. We learned about the true meaning of some rituals and customs. It was more than the groom with a kente cummerbund or the bride wearing a bridal gown with kente cloth woven in and a Baptist minister doing a European marriage ceremony and then jumping over a broom at the end. He helped us to understand that an African wedding is about the joining of two families instead of the joining of two people. All of the rituals leading up to the wedding were even more important. It helped me to become more ethnically centered and gave me a reason for establishing a family, and I had finally found the right girl, or so I thought.

The wedding ceremony went well. Through this process of learning, preparing, and doing I gained a better relationship with my kids, especially my daughter, not that we didn't have a good relationship before, but I began to understand why it was important for me, as a father, to have a good father–daughter relationship. I didn't need her going out into the world trying to find a father in a relationship. I was, am, and always will be her father. This, plus many other lessons I took away from the preparation of our wedding, showed us how to put our salon in place.

Our first salon had an African theme. Connie and I wore African garb, the shop was decorated with African prints, statues, colors, music, pictures, and candles, and we played prerecorded lectures on the television. The image of a husband and wife styling team, very ethnically centered and a magnetic atmosphere, brought in the people. Rich conversations and debates about relationships, social issues, finances, politics, and other struggles kept the time moving. The vibes and energy were very calming. My sister-in-law, who had a degree in fashion design, joined the business and we became "Hair Designer's Designer." One could have their hair and nails done, a dress made or altered, a wedding gown made, weddings planned, and many other things. Our shop attracted people from everywhere. Two in particular were Ruby and her friend Pam .

Chapter 6

THEY WERE BOTH TRUE IMAGES of very strong women. The two had moved down from Louisiana where they both came up and attended college together. Pam was the less spoken of the two, but when she did, it always came out in a burst of emotions. For anything that happened, no matter how big or small, this was how she expressed herself. "High yellow" with below shoulder-length hair, she was the total opposite of Ruby, who was dark chocolate, talkative, and very measured in her response.

Ruby was the ultimate businessperson. She was very organized and direct in her approach to everything, always wearing business suits neat and clean as if she had just walked out of the cleaners. She was very athletic; as a matter of fact, she had played basketball in high school and college. The fact that she worked out every day was the reason for her low body fat. She had a chiseled face with high cheekbones that gave her an almost Indian look, and a short, straight haircut that had her coming to the shop every week to keep it looking perfect. But what I thought was just her coming in to get her hair done, instead, was two women bonding. Bonding the way Connie and I bonded before we were married. Only they were more secretive, a lot more secretive. They were building a bond that would, eventually, break our bond.

Never did I know this would be my first look into the fact that my wife had a hidden secret. A secret that when exposed would change the lives of everyone around her, especially mine.

At first it seemed as though Ruby was a bother to Connie. She would call and, although I didn't know at the time—I would only hear the conversation from one end of the phone—flirt with her. I was under the impression that she got on Connie's nerves because of some of the things she would say about her calling all the time. But soon I started to see Connie on the phone all the time, even doing hair while talking on the phone. She would be laughing and walking around the house talking on the phone, driving the car and talking on the phone. My thought at first was, *Good! Connie has found a friend. A girl who she sees as a strong female.*

You see, women who don't depend on men always appealed to her. In our salon it was rare to find women who didn't appeal to her because most salon talk is about "no good men" or some woman complaining about how her man didn't treat her with attention or "My man can't keep a job so I have to have two jobs." But rarely was there talk about a woman who really didn't need a man. In the real sense of, "I don't need a man."

Connie would often say that her mother always taught them to never depend on men, which is a good principle to live by in theory: "Have your own money, car, job, and house." I'm sure her mother taught this because of her experience with men. She, too, had to deal with a marriage to a man who depended on her, but in return could not depend on him. I think Connie took it literally.

So part of her conversation was always about independence. It was not unusual to see Connie on her soapbox to all the women in the salon holding herself up to the world as a great example of a strong, independent woman. I guess for me as a husband, if that made her happy to see herself that way, then she was an independent woman.

Chapter 7

THE ONE INSTANCE WHEN IT occurred to me that something out of the ordinary was afoot was during our trip to Atlanta, Georgia. Every year, to bring in the New Year, a group of us would take a trip to Atlanta, and this year included our two new friends Ruby and Pam. We all crowded into one hotel room and used it for bathing and changing because we would not sleep.

Throughout the trip, Connie stuck close to Ruby. Just going shopping always led to Connie and Ruby being in one store together, while everyone else was shopping in another. I had convinced myself that Connie was just shopping with a girl who was her friend not a "girlfriend." Even when we went out to a club, often Connie and Ruby would end up on the dance floor together. But it's not uncommon for girls to dance together on the dance floor, so I didn't think much of it. I just continued having a good time with everybody else.

It all came to a head on the ride home when Ruby started flirting again. I was driving and Connie was sitting in the passenger's seat with Ruby sitting directly behind her. The music was on and everyone else was sleeping. But when things are quiet in a car, sound travels farther than you think.

Ruby leaned forward thinking she was whispering in Connie's ear, and in a voice that was dripping with the sexy sound of seduction, she asked slowly, "What would happen if I put relaxer on the hair around my vagina?" Somehow this sounded like foreplay to me, as I sat there stoned faced waiting to see Connie's reaction. I just knew she was about to give her some choice words. Instead she started to giggle like a little girl; I noticed she touched the inner part of her thigh as she crossed them and took a deep breath as she seemed to ponder just how to answer. I had never seen this side of her. Her slow reaction even made me take a deep breath. I guess the sound in a van really does bounce all over the place. Just the energy and reaction to that question made me very uncomfortable. By now I was clinching the steering wheel so tightly that I could feel the rotation of the tires through it.

With my heart beating fast, as I paused to calm myself down to only react in a verbal way, I said out loud with a huff, "It will burn the hell out of your pussy! What do you think will happen?"

At this point it was obvious that I could hear and was annoyed. The sound of my voice vibrated throughout the van and woke everybody out of his or her sleep. I think I was more bothered by Connie's reaction more so than the question, which was that she started to giggle as if to blush. Truth be told, even at this point the thought of Connie being a lesbian never entered my mind. For me, it felt kind of flirty and Ruby had gotten the reaction that she was seeking. You could tell by the sudden silence in the van that everybody else was surprised as well.

The rest of the ride home was not full of conversation, mostly small talk. Connie spent the rest of the trip part asleep and part laughing at things that were not as funny as her laughter; it became clear that a line had been crossed and that I was very annoyed. So for the rest of the trip home it remained quiet as everybody drifted off back to sleep. I guess it was good that I was the driver.

When we returned to Ft. Lauderdale, we dropped everyone off to his or her cars, which were left at the salon. Except for Clint, a friend who also went to Atlanta with us. His car was parked at our house. After we parked the van at our house and started to unpack—pressure is a hell of a thing—Connie passed out. Clint and I, in a panic, picked her up, put her in the van, and started driving toward the hospital. I was driving down sidewalks, down one-way streets the wrong way, making U-turns in the middle of the streets, trying to get to the hospital. Strange though, the closer I got to the hospital the more I realized my wife was faking to take the heat and focus off of our trip to Atlanta and the things that happened when we were there. Things were starting to come together.

One funny thing that happened that made me feel that she was putting on an Academy Award performance was Clint panicked and for no reason he said, "Let's take off her clothes so she can breathe." I don't know why, and neither did he. But it made sense at that moment.

We proceeded to try to take her tight pants off, and she grabbed them to stop us. But she was supposed to be passed out! Passed out but aware, hmmm...now how does that work? Clint had no interest in seeing her naked; he was gay. Now, I know that doesn't mean that a gay man wouldn't want to see a woman naked, but in this case this one didn't.

After going through all the different tests, it was just as I believed: everything was fine. Thinking that she was just going through curiosity and boredom as some relationships go through, thinking that it would fade away as something that just happened, I let her have that one and never brought it up again. I wish I could explain my feelings or my choice of not confronting her with my thoughts, but even to this day I still don't have an answer.

About a few days later, we were in the shop one night when Ruby stopped by to apologize to me for what had happened. Connie, for some reason, came over to tell her everything was okay but tried to slip a note in her hand that read: "I'll call you later." But the note dropped, I picked it up, and read it. I was outraged at the deception and stormed out the door, followed by my best friend Herman. I got into my car to go home and get my clothes to leave. By the time I got home and started packing, Connie and her mom were pulling up. Connie started to pull me into the bedroom yelling, "It's not what you think!"

I said, "I know what I saw!" I started to realize that they were together more than just at the shop or around me.

Gary Cooper

For some reason, she pulled me into the shower and turned the water on. We were standing in the cold shower in our clothes, shoes and all, with her trying to calm me and convince me that she was just going through something and that it was done. She said the only reason for the note was to let Ruby know that she had only friendly intentions. And that this was all just girl stuff. I guess some people are good salesmen because, let's face it, in marriages you are constantly negotiating your point of view, and I don't know too many people who could sell their vision of what just happened better than Connie. Girl stuff and women's problem is one thing men have no idea about, and anytime we hear it we shut down and say okay. It's like that thing in the glass case that you break out: when all else fails break glass. So just like swirling wine around in a nice wine glass to stir up the aromas, I swirled that logic around in my head, and suddenly it made sense to me. Matter of fact, by now I started thinking maybe I was tripping. I guess I was ready to give her the benefit of the doubt, and so I did. Now I was too exhausted to take it any further.

After driving all the way from Georgia and going right back to work, I needed sleep and that's what I did, got some sleep.

Don't think I was crazy; I was just a man trying to make sense out of what was going on. A man trying to make sense of something that didn't make sense. Somehow we got through that night. Only because she convinced me that I was overreacting and that she was trying to let Ruby know not come around us again. After that night she didn't.

I woke up the next morning feeling better but not sure of my trust in my wife. I guess within the next few days she helped me to feel that her fantasy was over and done. I'll admit, she did everything to show me I could trust her. She even threw me a surprise birthday party, and we weekended together in Palm Beach and Orlando. When we got back, we got busy putting together a hair and fashion show.

The show kept us occupied and got us back into African culture. Life was starting to get back to normal. Every once in a while the subject of, "Are you a lesbian?" would come up.

But this question would always be greeted with anger. "How many times do I have to keep answering that question? I already told you no. Can't we ever get past that?" would be her response.

Well, after a while hearing that response enough will make you tired of asking. But years from now I would find out so much more about this entire episode. At that time, I was more concerned about getting our life back to normal.

Chapter 8

THEY SAY TIME HEALS ALL wounds, so in time our life was back on track, at least for the next few years. It was during this year that my wife got a reading from our spiritual advisor. One day she came to me and told me that our ancestral reading said we should have a child together. I guess, at first I was taken aback. But later I had so much fun trying to have a baby on purpose; we had sex all the time. Sex with a purpose.

For a while I was worried because with all the trying, we weren't getting pregnant. I was wondering if the reading was correct. Then one month I noticed that she missed her period. Could this be it? Or was I jumping the gun? I didn't want to get too excited because that had happened before when her period was only late. I didn't like seeing her so disappointed, or me feeling disappointed either for that matter. So this time we waited and waited. We both walked around on pins and needles. After about two months of missing her cycle we went to the doctor to be told what we had already figured out, that we were pregnant. You can imagine how elated I was. This was a feeling that I had never experienced—having a baby on purpose. Neither had she for that matter. We were about to burst with joy. After all that hard "work"…and I say that with a smile. The reality of new life was real, and so started a new chapter in our ever-evolving life.

The process of going through a pregnancy was easy for us. We were self-employed and owned our own business. We were used to working together in everything else, so working through a pregnancy was no different. Connie had a pretty easy pregnancy, if there is such a thing. We were able to travel, have sex, and everything else. Toward the end there were a few complications with the pregnancy. But even those complications were just minor bumps that gave us a chance to take it easy, seeing that we were always doing things.

Then on December 28, 1995, Boy Cooper was born. I will never forget the look on Connie's face when she saw him for the first time. I really can't put it into words to describe it. I had seen that look in her eyes before at times of great joy. Like the day that we walked into our first house or walked into our first very nice apartment and realized it was a loft. Boy Cooper came into the world like a bolt of lightning; he was delivered by C-section. But once the nurse took him and cleaned him up, what was before us was a little Asian, alien-looking baby. I stared at him trying to focus on him. I looked at him sideways, examining his toes, head, and eyes. When I got to his fingers I stopped and paused. My eyes focused on his fingers. He had an extra finger on each hand. Seems this runs in my family on my father's side. Thinking back, my sister and my father's sister, my aunt, had an extra finger at birth as well. My sister had a little bump on her pinky finger. And with Boy Cooper, even though we got his lanced (string tied around it to cut it off), for me that was a sign of my family's spirit still circulating in my life. As far as I was concern, I was so happy to have an old spirit come back.

He came in crying, looking around with a look about him that said, "Strap in and get ready for one hell of a ride." The nurse took him and laid him in Connie's arms. I could tell from the look in her eyes that she was amazed that this is what had been kicking in her stomach for all these months. This is one of the rare times that I got to see a soft side of Connie. We sat there and just stared at our little alien for what seemed like forever.

For the moment, I think we felt like a family. I think that was the purpose for having a baby in the first place, to bring our family closer together. During that time I saw no signs of her wanting to be with anybody but our newborn son and me. I think she thought this would tame the feeling inside that was calling out to her concerning her sexual interest in women. But one thing is never the substitute for another. It's all still there. Just like a beautiful gift wrapped in a box with a big bowtie and tag saying, "wait to open." But for now I think bringing this spirit into the world was more important than sexuality. So we just enjoyed this moment, looking at our little Boy Cooper.

We took him out of the hospital as Boy Cooper, after which we had a naming ceremony and he was given the name N'kosi, which means "ruler." And boy, did he live up to his name! I guess I became attached to his spirit and he to mine because where I went, he went.

I remember when we would come home at night I would be in the bathroom and he would sit outside the bathroom on the floor and play with his toys until I got out of the bathroom. When I would yell out to him to go downstairs with his mother or grandmother, he would always yell back, "I'm okay."

When we renewed our vows on our second honeymoon to Jamaica, he came with us. For me that was the best part of the honeymoon— going to the market, the beach, and the different sights in Jamaica with my wife and son. I guess for the first time, I felt like a family man and husband.

Chapter 9

N'KOSI BROUGHT STABILITY TO OUR life. Even though Michael and Jermaine had been there as our sons, N'kosi gave us balance. With Connie raising Michael when she was a young person pursuing modeling and partying in between, it didn't give her a lot of time to raise him as a day-to-day mother. With me running around trying to make it in the music business having custody of my son, Jermaine, most of his raising was done by my mom and aunts; that didn't really qualify me as a day-to-day father. You see, I also had two other sons, Cory and Koran, and a daughter, Joy, who would spend the weekends with us. It was still safe to say I wasn't much of a father. But for both Connie and me, N'kosi was our chance to really raise a child and truly be parents. It was our chance to become the family we both wanted, plus his spirit was a welcomed addition to our really routine lives.

Raised around the salon by so many people, N'kosi became used to being around many types of people, so he wanted to do the things that he saw everybody else do. Like starting to walk by seven months, seeing me pee standing up and keep my hand on to shake the drip off, and wanting underwear instead of diapers. He was a child who was comfortable around anybody. His personality and dreadlocks gave him opportunities for castings and print ads where he almost always got a part. This went on until it was no longer fun for him. At that point, we stopped taking him to the castings.

By this time, we had moved our salon to a new location. This was a salon that we renovated ourselves. It had cobwebs, old stoves, fridges, air conditioners—basically a condemned restaurant was renovated with my own hands. I renovated the entire restaurant into a beautiful salon. From the walls to the floor, I built everything.

Soon our new salon was up and running. We had gone through a few assistants and soon hired a girl who helped us with hair in the Hair and Fashion Show, for the grand reopening of our newly renovated salon, Her name was Tasha. Tasha was a tall, leggy, mocha chocolate girl. At the time she had medium-length hair that she wore in a bob style but would soon trade in for dreadlocks. She was very chesty, and she had the most beautiful full lips I had ever seen. In no time flat, it felt as if she had been with us for years. It would be a few years later before I'd realize how important she would be in my life.

I guess for the most part, our family was like most. But fast forward a few years and things began to change.

Chapter 10

IN 2003, AN OLD FRIEND and customer, Lisa, came by the shop. It was not odd for her to come hang out at the shop; it was the kind of place where people felt comfortable hanging out and talking. But there was something different about this time. I got the feeling that she was trying to wait for all the customers to leave. I thought it had something to do with trouble at home. We finished the last few heads, sent them out the door, and soon we were the only three left in the shop. She and I sat in the chairs up front, and Connie sat behind the counter to close out the cash register, but she was still within earshot of us. It became quiet and still, as if the moment was waiting for what's next. There was a kind of nervousness surrounding us as she started trying to find the right words to start off whatever was bothering her. I looked over at her and she took a deep breath as if she had just told herself, "I'm just going to go for broke" and came up with the words, "I don't want you to hear this in the streets. I don't want you to hear this from anyone but me." When you hear those words I don't care what you are doing, you stop. It gets your attention. Connie stopped what she was doing and came over and joined us. She looked at us both, and you could tell she was still searching for the words. She tried again. "I've gone the other way."

I looked at her, puzzled. "The other way?" I asked.

"Yes," she said. Then she took another deep breath and kind of stared off as if she was still searching for the words. Then it just came out in one big burst. "I have been having a relationship with another woman, and I am in love with her." She stopped almost as if she was surprised to hear those words coming from her own mouth. It was as if in that moment she became energized. She sat straight up, looked at us both, and said in a more assured voice, "I want you to know I am out of the closet. And the more honest I became with myself, the more I realized that I've felt this way long before I met somebody."

She had been married for years, and she and her husband had a son. But the marriage had come to the point where they weren't even sleeping in the same bedroom. She told us this had gone on for about a year until one night she just wanted to get out of the house. She went for a drive and decided to stop at a local bar and pool hall. As she sat at the bar to have a drink she noticed a girl at the table shooting pool, and pretty soon the two were making small talk.

About half an hour later, she challenged the girl to a game; the loser would buy the next round of drinks. She said they were just shooting, drinking, and talking till soon she realized that hours had gone by and not once did the thought of her husband come to mind. As a matter of fact, she couldn't remember the last time she felt so comfortable talking to someone. But more importantly, with this person there was something more about her that she couldn't get out of her head. And even though at the end of the night they hugged and said good night, one side of her was saying, *I must be going crazy.* She went home, lay in bed, and replayed that night in her head till the next morning. Even by then she couldn't get the girl off her mind. And that's why she knew she had to see her again.

That encounter started something that she never ever considered before—a romantic relationship with a woman. Every day they would talk on the phone on and off almost all day. Flirting, bonding, and touching her soul through words. Waking up parts of her that she didn't know existed, making her fill like a teenager all over again. Now she couldn't wait to see her, to the point where when her husband would get home from work she would be waiting for him just so he could watch their son. The minute he walked in she would be out the door.

The girl's name was Kelly, and just the way Kelly touched her woke up every sensation in her body. We made a joke about her tingling all day. I could tell by the excitement in her eyes that she was happier than she had ever been in her entire life. It was as if she had been reintroduced to herself.

I remember us hugging her and telling her that she deserved to be happy because she was such a good person with a good spirit. Both Connie and I told her we'd be there for her. We felt honored that it was so important to her to tell us personally. But if I had paid attention I would have noticed Connie's silence during most of Lisa's story. It was as if she was in deep thought the whole time. What was she thinking about? I didn't know and she wasn't saying. In most cases, she would have been a lot more involved, but now she seemed more of a listener. It was getting late so soon we said our good-byes and Connie and I finished cleaning up the shop and left for home.

A few days passed and Lisa brought her friend Kelly over to introduce her to us. From what I could see, she was a good person who had really experienced life. She was dressed in dark clothes and she had a short, boyish haircut, dyed blonde. She had a gapped tooth but somehow on her it was sexy. Maybe it was because she had a Trinidadian accent, but the way she framed her words made you take note of every word she spoke. A kind of flirty fun way of expressing herself is about as close as I can explain. She was a charmer and I could see why Lisa would be drawn to her, because she had a way of making you feel like you've known her all your life. She brought needed excitement to Lisa's life. Little did I know she would bring so much to ours, as well.

Soon we began to do things together like going to dinner, breakfast, each other's homes, and to parties. At that time, I saw their commitment to each other. They were as committed as any other couple. By now I didn't even see them as a lesbian couple; to us they were just another couple.

Gary Cooper

One day Lisa invited us, along with Tasha, over to their house for her birthday party. That was one of the first times that the setting was all lesbians, except for my wife, Tasha, and me. At first I didn't know how to feel or act. But in no time flat it became like any other party with the exception of my being the only man, but that made no difference. Being the only man at a party with so many women is a dream that most men have or have had. But for those men it would have been just that, a dream. Not one woman here would have been interested. But other than that, just like any other party, everybody was there to have a good time. And just like any other party there were many kind of women, some masculine, some feminine, big, small, skinny, wealthy, almost poor, doctors, plus a lawyer or two. Throughout the night, I got a chance to talk to different women and learn more about who they were and, most importantly, why they were here. There were lessons all over the place, and this was the beginning of laying the groundwork for lessons for all of us.

I was just at a party, soaking up the food, music, and good conversation, and I guess at the time I never thought about everyone's coming-out stories. And believe me there were some. You see, some came from marriages with kids, husbands, and families trying to fit into other people's views of who to love and how to live, sometimes fearing their response to who they were or who they chose to have a relationship with. I mean, some were like outcasts in their families. So together in this setting, they were truly free to be themselves. Now that's not to say that everyone was misunderstood by their family members. All had stories of their own of how they came out, and their own struggles to be free. Some started out by totally rejecting their lifestyle but over time came to deal with or accept it. And some, because of their religious beliefs, never could deal with it, even though the Bible says, "Love your (neighbor) brother as you would yourself." I guess there are a lot of self-hating people in the world.

That would be the first of many gatherings we would attend, and I mean we went from one party to another. I can't say that the entire lesbian lifestyle is like this, but we were going out two or three nights a week. Soon we became part of the clique. I have to admit that life had become very exciting and liberating for us, and I'm straight. When you go to lesbian clubs you see a part of life that you never realized was there—women from all walks of life dancing, drinking, talking, and romancing with no one to judge them. If I had noticed, I would have realized that my wife was beginning to change. She seemed to be more comfortable or relaxed in this setting, and we all began to become joined at the hip. Even when Lisa and Kelly moved into a new house, we were there to help them move. We all painted together. I put all the blinds up, replaced the pool pump, and did anything else we could do.

In that same year, I got together with my old music group to do a benefit reunion concert for Mecca. Victor, a former group member who had become a minister and activist, headed Mecca. With great sponsors, this charity gave scholarships to underprivileged kids.

Chapter 11

IT TOOK A LOT OF practice to sound like a band again. I would leave from the salon at night and go straight to practice in Hollywood, Florida, leaving Connie at the shop. She would then go over to Lisa's house. When I would get out of practice, she would still be there. I attributed that to her not knowing the exact time I would be getting home from rehearsal. I never wondered about what they did when they were together. They were friends chillin'. Just like it is when I visit my friend. We'll do a lot of things but one thing was for sure; there wouldn't be anything romantic going on between me and any man! And I thought Connie felt the same way.

Soon it got to the point where she would spend all her time over there. It was hard to get her to spend much time at home. Our life became consumed with partying from house party to house party. Even after the benefit concert, she wanted to go out afterward with Lisa, Kelly, and another friend. I was too mentally drained. She really wanted to go, so I told her I didn't mind if she went without me. I went home and told the friend who was babysitting N'kosi I could take it from here. She left, I took a shower, and went to bed. Somewhere around three in the morning I fell asleep, not even giving a second thought about her going out, meeting some man, and complicating our marriage. I'm pretty sure I kind of dozed in and out, seeing that I was mentally drained from all the rehearsing, and the eventual show.

When she got home, there was a strange vibe about her that I just thought came from being tired. I remember lying in bed and being awakened by the sound of the garage door opening, her car pulling in, and the car door slamming. I could hear the sound of her feet walking up the stairs and slowly opening the bedroom door. I lay with my back facing her so she probably couldn't see that I was awake.

She went into the bathroom, washed up, and came to bed. I'm used to her backing up close to me; she would always say it made her feel safe. But this night she stayed on her side of the bed, with the space between us so big that you could drive a Humvee between us. I figured she was just tired. All I saw was Connie going out with three girlfriends. I didn't see it as a lesbian thing. I never even wondered what happened that night or why she didn't snuggle up to me like she usually did. Somewhere along the line we both dozed off. But from this night, it fast-forwarded into a series of events that changed all of our lives; we just didn't realize it yet, but things were about to move very fast.

The next month we went to New York for Gay Pride Week to support Lisa, Kelly, and other lesbian couples' right to be what made them happy. The month leading up to Pride Week, I saw Connie becoming more excited about going. Even though we were going to Jamaica first, Jamaica didn't matter. It was New York that mattered most. Not just New York, but I now realized it was Pride Week in New York. I still didn't see the connection.

Flying to New York, I had a feeling of anticipation, which I didn't understand. We were excited for two different reasons. I knew the reason *I* was excited, and I hoped that Connie was excited for the same reason.

Arriving in New York for Pride Week was something to behold—an entire city being part of, and welcoming, gays and lesbians from all walks of life. I mean clubs, restaurants, clothing stores, and hotels in the entire city all became a part of this week. What you saw was freedom to be who you were. We had so much fun that I didn't realize that we were having fun for two different reasons: 1) I was there to help celebrate Lisa being able to be herself, and 2) my wife was having so much fun being comfortable around so many people being who they were. Sometimes it almost felt as if I wasn't there, or it would have been better for her if I weren't there. I guess the old phrase "When a person shows you who they are, believe them" should have spoken to me, but I was totally oblivious to what was going on around me. I guess I was so happy for Lisa that I was just enjoying myself seeing her enjoying herself. I could see why Pride Week was so life changing for so many.

Though there's one big parade on Sunday to cap off the week, there were many parties all over the city every day and night. The parties included all women or all men. Of all the parties I attended, I was basically the only man. At times, I felt like a kid in a candy store with a pocket full of dimes. But I knew different; I was in New York celebrating Gay Pride Week at a lesbian party with my wife and our lesbian friends. What's so abnormal about that? To tell you the truth, it didn't seem to matter. At times I danced with a line of women. It anchored my belief that people are people. The fact that I was a heterosexual male made no difference. Both friends and strangers treated Connie and me like man and wife. I had no thought of any woman there wanting my wife. Probably because it's like any other club setting; some couples had committed relationships like my wife and me, and some were single.

But Connie's attitude was changing. I was constantly getting separated from her, and I got the feeling that she wasn't trying to find me. For instance, one day, which I believe was on a Saturday, Lisa wanted to take Connie shopping for shoes at Macy's in Manhattan. This was Connie's second time being in New York, and her first time being there like this— no kids or family. When Lisa asked us to come, Connie intercepted my reply, "He's going to be too bored, 'cause he knows how I get when I shop for shoes." Well, she was right. I hated to go shopping with her.

So I said, "You three go. I'll get some things done and look up some old friends. I'll call you when I get back; hopefully you'll be done."

"Okay," she replied. And with that they left.

After about three hours I called Connie's cell phone, but no answer. I waited about thirty or forty minutes. No answer. By now I was getting annoyed so I started to walk toward Macy's but couldn't find them.

About an hour later I ran into them walking down thirty 6th Street, and boy was I pissed.

Lisa and Kelly really had no idea why I was so pissed, but Connie knew exactly why. Sounding very angry I asked, "Why didn't you pick up the phone?"

She replied, "The phone was in my pocketbook and I couldn't hear it."

"But after all these hours didn't it dawn on you that maybe you need to check up on Gary, or at least touch bases with him?" I responded.

"I was so busy shopping that I lost track of time," she said.

By then I was too pissed to talk about it or I would have started to yell. So I turned around and we started to walk back to the hotel. The whole time Connie was still explaining how she didn't hear the phone and how she was so excited by all the shoes. The clues were there and they were coming from everywhere, but I still wasn't seeing them.

Later, Lisa said to me, "Don't say anything but even *I* kept hearing her phone, so I don't know how *she* couldn't hear it."

By the end of the day I had put the thing behind me for the sake of the trip. A husband's mind-set I guess. I've often heard the saying, "love is blind," and in hindsight, I was blind. Once again, my thoughts at the time were that she was just having a good time.

Sunday was the last day for the parade, which was a gathering of all people, straight, gay, and lesbian. You name it and they were there. If you ever questioned your sexuality, this would be the place to get the answer, or at least begin to search.

After we returned from New York, life had changed. Connie seemed so invigorated. We would spend all our time either at Lisa's and Kelly's house, or at one of their friend's houses, a party, lesbian club, movie, dinner, breakfast, or almost any lesbian event. I guess at the time I couldn't tell you why I was there. I still wasn't putting it together. I still never wondered why we were attending all of these lesbian affairs. I guess I still looked at the four of us as two couples doing things together.

One day Connie started to repeat rumors she was told by a friend of ours. For example, in the entertainment business, Will and Jada Smith's successful marriage was due to the fact that Jada was lesbian and that people in those circles knew this. (She was speaking to the fact that I had so much respect for their relationship and how they treated each other.) Soon I would understand why she was trying to plant those things in my mind. Of course, no one told her that. But I guess she was trying to make me believe our relationship would be better if she could experiment.

This would be the first of many ways that she would try to experience sex with another woman and get my blessing. Things like wanting to bring another woman into our bed. Not for me, but for herself. But of course it wasn't presented that way. It was always presented as a "serious joke" in order to see how I would respond. But now I understand why she wanted to try this fantasy. I tell men all the time now that if your wife ever asks you about bringing another woman for a threesome, before you get excited you should know it's for her, not for you. Why? Well, she knows what it feels to have sex with you but may not know what it feels like to have sex with another woman, and may be curious. This way she gets your blessing as well as your participation, sort of like now your hands are dirty too. So be prepared for what could happen after. Still, as a husband, I guess I hoped this would pass. I still didn't understand what was happening, but it was becoming very stressful.

Soon Connie spent most of her time on the phone, which was reminiscent of our encounter years before. But this time was different. The person on the other end of the line was no longer Lisa and Kelly. It became just Kelly. As I recall, several things happened that led up to the climactic end. I noticed that for no reason at all Connie started to drink iced coffee from Dunkin Donuts every morning. I know it doesn't mean much, but this was Kelly's favorite drink. I still hadn't put it together yet, but for some reason I noticed, so it must have been an important sign; there was something about it that stuck with me. Then there were times that she would come home smelling like men's cologne. But sometimes you meet people out and embrace them so it was no big deal, until I passed by Kelly one night and recognized that same smell. Once again, I noticed but didn't think much about it. I know you must be saying, "What does it take, a dump truck to hit him?" Well, keep reading and you will see a dump truck did. Or at least it felt like it did.

The next was the MTV Street Party in Miami. Her behavior became so out of control that I demanded that we leave. Connie had too much to drink; I had never seen her drunk before. I really went off, to the point that Kelly tried to calm me. Lisa hugged Connie to help her to the car. But even Lisa had no idea that Kelly had a lot to do with what was going on. Since we were all riding together with other friends of Kelly and Lisa's, we left thinking that we were going home. Instead, we ended up at a lesbian club. Another lesbian club. The bells are ringing, the lights are flashing, and the sirens are blasting, but still, I'm not getting it.

At this club, Connie stayed on the dance floor dancing with many people, acting drunker than she really was. At some point we left and went home. I guess by now my mouth was void of words because I didn't know what to say or even what to think. I know one might ask why I was still allowing myself to be around them. The only answer for me would be, "I don't know." I mean, maybe by now it seemed that I was starting to notice that the so-called aggressive lesbians were circling Connie like buzzards around a dead carcass, or maybe the dead carcass had committed suicide in order to be eaten.

I thought Connie needed to get all the excitement of that lifestyle out of her system, and in the meantime my presence would give boundaries to anybody with any other motives. That it would say, "I'm married to this man, so don't even think about it." Boy was I wrong!

By now Connie had a telephone attached to her ear, because she was always on it, always talking to Kelly, always laughing and whispering. She was barely coming to the salon. Whereas before, my routine was to get up in the morning, get N'kosi dressed for school, get him breakfast, take him to school, and go to the shop to open by 9:00 a.m. Connie would do things around the house like clean, do laundry, pay bills, and then come to the shop between 11:00 a.m. and 12:00 p.m. And now her behavior was changing.

Chapter 12

ONE DAY CONNIE CAME TO the shop with her navel pierced—not that there's anything wrong with piercing your navel. For her, things like that or tattoos were always frowned upon. Never mind it just popped up, and I never heard prior that she wanted to do a piercing of any kind. I always thought that before married people did something as drastic as that they would talk about it first. She was getting to the shop later and later, and not picking up her phone. At times she would have her phone vibrate and would keep checking it. This was evident the night we went to a '70s party.

Connie's women's group was having a party one Saturday night in 2004. It was a fundraiser. All week long, putting together the event and coming up with the '70s outfits was more fun than the party itself. On the evening of the party, I left the salon last to give Connie time to go to the house to get ready while I finished the last customer and closed the shop. On the way home, I called to let her know that I was heading home and to make sure she was just about dressed. She didn't pick up. After calling about two more times I figured she was just taking a shower.

When I got home, I went upstairs and heard her answer the phone. It was Tasha calling, but it dawned on me that the phone never rang. At least, I never heard it ring. I didn't give it much thought. I asked, "Why is your phone on silent?"

Playing dumb, she said, "I didn't know it was. I must have put it on by mistake."

I really didn't go any further with the why, I just said, "Well, let's hurry up and get dressed so that we are not late." We got dressed and left.

On our way to the party I started to notice that Connie had an attitude and seemed distant and angry. When I asked her what was wrong she snapped at me and said, "Why are you questioning me?"

"I'm just trying to figure out what's going on with you," I shot back.

"Well, I was doing fine until you started questioning me."

All of this came out of nowhere. Next thing I knew we were pulling into the parking lot of the party. We had fussed all the way there.

Looking back, I realize the arguing was both her feeling anxious and frustrated that one, Kelly was with Lisa, and two, that she had to wait for Kelly to contact her because she couldn't call her.

At the party, we didn't spend a lot of time together. It was more like she was entertaining over here while I was doing the same over there. Everyone was wondering why she kept going to her pocketbook to check her phone. She seemed distant and stressed trying to juggle her secret.

At the end of the night we said good-bye to everybody and left to go home. The ride home was quiet because I didn't know how to talk to her without getting into an argument. She was frustrated and I was mentally drained and didn't know that things were about to really get weird.

The moment that changed everything started one Saturday in September of 2004. That night we went to the housewarming party of a friend of Lisa's. This friend was straight, but one of the women had eyes for her and was trying to make a move. I was there at the party, but my mind wasn't, and neither was Connie's. It was obvious that something was not right. We left the party feeling the same way, with very few words. When we got home we had a half talk, which seemed more like me trying to pull information out of her about what was going on. Even then she couldn't come out with the words, "I am a lesbian." It was made out to be more like "I'm curious." For the most part though, we both lay around staring at nothing, us both with apposing thoughts that made us both seem disconnected from each other. For the first time since we've been together, I felt as if I was sitting in bed with a stranger. I'm pretty sure if I could read her mind she was feeling the same way. Without saying much after that, we fell asleep.

The next morning, the phone ringing awakened us. It was Lisa. They too had been up that night talking and wanted to go to breakfast to talk to us. By the time we got dressed, they were there to pick us up. We mostly laughed and talked about other things until we got to the restaurant. Connie and Lisa got a table outside while Kelly and I got breakfast. After which we all sat down to enjoy breakfast together. I remember how nice the weather was prior to our eating, a very clear but cool morning. I guess the universe knew that we would need some sunshine really soon.

Lisa looked up with a very serious and concerned look on her face and asked what was wrong. "When we started coming around, you two were so happy, and I would hate to think that we had something to do with the change. I'm just concerned and want to know the truth," she said. Lisa and Kelly were sitting across from us, with Kelly directly in front of me. First there was silence.

Then Connie looked up and said, "You want the truth, then I'll give you the truth. The truth is I've fallen in love with Kelly!"

Silence. It was like time froze for about sixty seconds. No one knew what to say. I got ready to stop Lisa from jumping over the table and choking Connie because I just knew I was going to have to pull her off. But I think she was too shocked to move.

I waited for Kelly to speak of her part in this matter because I had already figured her feelings were mutual and this had been going on for quite some time. This would help explain all the missing moments, all the phone calls. I had answered quite a few of the calls myself, spoke for a few moments, and then would tell Connie, "Telephone, it's Kelly." All I saw was a friend on the other end. It just never dawned on me otherwise. Now, I knew for sure. She said it herself.

51

We all sat there dumbfounded and no one knew what to say. Lisa looked over at Kelly, and in a voice that was obviously trembling from part hurt and part confusion, asked, "Did you know anything about this?"

Kelly's eyes darted back and forth between Lisa and me as if she was just as shocked as we were. Now that I reflect back, I realize that she never did answer. It was more of an assortment of sounds that really didn't make much sense, sort of the kind you make when you try but can't come up with the right words. It was at that moment that I was more than sure that she did. I wish I could say that something exciting happened at this point other than silence, but by now I figured it was time to leave. There was a strange kind of vibration that fell over all of us, so Kelly and I went and paid our bill while Lisa and Connie walked back to the car. Connie was walking behind Lisa, and I soon I caught up with Connie, because I just knew that Lisa was going to reach over and choke Connie who was more than likely feeling justified about being honest. Yes, Connie always championed herself on being honest, but that was only if that honesty was to her benefit. She looked over and asked Lisa, "What do you want me to do?"

"Stay the fuck away from us, bitch," Lisa replied with disgust in her face. She looked over to me and asked, "Are you okay?"

"Yeah," I replied, but really I was numb. It was as if I had been in a fight with Mike Tyson and had been hit so hard that I didn't know where I was. Just dazed.

When we got to the car we had to stand around the car waiting for Kelly to reach us with the keys. Looking in with the door opened, I realized we couldn't have the same seating arrangement that we had coming. So I reversed that by putting Connie directly behind Lisa, so that she couldn't see her unless she turned around, and I knew that was not likely.

Driving home was very quiet. The only words that I can remember was Connie whispering to me, "I guess I really messed up huh?"

"Yeah it's safe to say you really did," I replied. But all I kept thinking was *Man, this ride home is long* and *Did it take this long to get to the restaurant?*

When we got home Lisa was in tears. I remember thinking, *I wouldn't want to be Kelly riding home right now.* Lisa got out and hugged me. She was so disgusted she couldn't even look at Connie. She got back inside the car and pulled off .I stood for a minute to try to separate myself from what had just happened, because I knew that going back into my house was never going to be the same. And looking at Connie was going to be worse. So I took a deep breath, walked up the walkway, opened the door, and walked in.

Chapter 13

BEING INSIDE OUR HOUSE FELT strange. I didn't know where to sit, what to say, or even what to do. I just felt blank, numb. One part of me was angry. Another part of me felt sorry for Connie. When you care about someone you never want to see him or her hurt, even if it hurts you. So we kind of drifted throughout the house.

At the time I still didn't understand the full scope of what had taken place. I think her struggle was more than just feeling like she loved Kelly or that she had been sneaking around with her. Or even that she was ready to come out of the closet. Her problem was how to do it without being inconvenienced. After reflection, I think that bothered me most.

She came into the room where I was staring at the TV trying to figure out how to fix what couldn't be fixed. And for the next twenty-four hours we did a string of things that I couldn't and still can't explain. For some reason, she wanted to go to the beach or be around some water. So we got N'kosi, some towels, and a blanket and went to the beach. Lying on a blanket at the beach with the sun shining on my face did little to erase the feeling inside that I couldn't describe—still mostly blank and numb. We left the beach soon and went home.

The next day we took N'kosi to the park to watch him ride his bike. That night we popped popcorn and the three of us watched a movie. In all of this, we said very little to each other. Matter of fact, I can't remember anything we talked about. It was almost like a twenty-four hour dream. I guess Connie was trying to do all the things to convince herself of how important her family was.

After those two days, I was half convinced that maybe things could at some point get back to, not normal, but livable. I know this sounds delusional, but I didn't know how else to feel, so I went back to work.

We started back on the same schedule. I got up and took N'kosi to school and went to the salon. Connie got there between 11:00 a.m. and 12:00 p.m., but we would talk on the phone in between—I guess she knew that I no longer trusted her and wanted me to know she was home. After the first week, there were days that were reminiscent of the week before—missing time frames, the smell of cologne that I remembered.

One morning we didn't have everything needed to make breakfast, and I was going to go to the store to get them. Connie jumped up like this was her day to play the good wife and go to the store instead. "I'll go because I need to pick up some things to cook for dinner later anyway." She put on her clothes and left. I thought that everything was trying to move in the right direction.

After about an hour and a half I realized, *Man, she should be back by now, I hope everything is okay.* So I called her to check. No answer, straight to voice mail. So I waited about twenty more minutes, still no answer. I thought, *Maybe she got in an accident.* I got in the car because the store was right up the street and only one way to go. I traced the drive right up to the store; there was no Connie or her car. I thought maybe I missed her and passed her, so I went back to the house. Still no Connie.

By now I was a mixture of angry and concerned. What I did next I'm almost embarrassed to say, but I called Lisa. "Hello, Lisa?"

"Yes, how are you doing, and do you feel any better?"

"Yes just trying to put this all behind me," I said. "I just want you and Kelly to not be effected by what happened. Is she around?"

"Yes, she's in the kitchen. I'll have to see how this plays out with us."

"Well, just remember I am still your friend and if you ever need me just call."

"You the same," she said. With that we hung up.

The reason I did that was because I guess I just wanted to know if Kelly was home so that I could rule out that that's where Connie was. But that also explained her behavior when she did return home about an hour later. I heard the garage door opening and her car pull in. Not to seem like I was overreacting I just watched her walk into the house. From where I was sitting, and for the first time, I noticed how much weight she had lost. Her black jeans that once looked like she had been poured into them were now fitting like warm-up pants. She looked stressed, and it appeared that she had been crying. Of course that got my attention, and I walked over, hugged her, and asked her, "What's wrong?" I had forgotten to say, "Where have you been?" I was more concerned about why she was crying. I took her handbag from her hands and put it on the table then led her over to the chair and sat her down. Visibly shaken, stressed, and crying, she looked up at me and apologized. Sobbing, she said, "I just needed to get away by myself for a little while and think."

If not for the fact that I knew that Kelly was home with Lisa, I would have questioned her on that need. But at the time I didn't understand that, that was exactly the reason. Kelly was home with Lisa, and Connie was calling her to ask if she could get out of the house because she need to see her. Of course at the time I didn't know; I was concerned about what was wrong. She was holding her stomach and rocking herself. Seeing her that out of control was strange for me. Connie was one of those kinds of people who had to always have control, and I had never seen her like this. She kept saying her stomach was hurting in a way that she had never felt before. I felt helpless because I knew that I couldn't do anything to make her feel better.

For some reason, she picked up her bag and said she needed to go to the bathroom. But I pulled her bag from her hands, and the unzipped opening exposed that it was filled with bottles of pills. I stopped her and asked her, "What are the pills for?"

"I don't want to be here anymore," she said, and started pulling the bag.

We wrestled with the bag, and with one great pull I got the bag from her hand and poured all the pills on the floor. With the pills laying on the floor and her standing there sobbing, not quite knowing what to do, I poured the pills into the toilet and took her upstairs and laid her in the bed. I didn't know if I should call the paramedics, her family, or what. But by this time she seemed to have stopped crying.

I looked at her and said to her. "Whatever you are going through, killing yourself isn't the answer."

She just shook her head saying, "I know."

That answer was the opening for us to sit and have a reasonable talk about how she felt .She said she felt overwhelmed and anxious. I agreed with her that this had been a crazy two weeks, but somehow we had to get through it. She said, "I hope so." I had no idea how important that word *hope* would be.

I realized that she was dozing off, so I said, "Get some sleep" and pulled the cover up, kissed her on the forehead, and left the room. Maybe not the best way to handle it, but I too was feeling the same way, but for another reason.

For the next few days, I walked around in a daze. And for the next few days it seemed we held on to each other a little closer. I had no idea how different I would look at that scene in about another year. Things were about to get even crazier.

By midweek, the end of September 2004, we got a report that a hurricane was in the Atlantic Ocean, heading our way. A client of ours offered to give us her panel storm shutters because our houses were built by the same developer and was similar in dimensions. Her husband didn't always feel like putting up the panels, so they had recently installed sliding shutters.

On Friday, we knew that by Saturday night the hurricane was going to be on us. So Friday night I told Connie that I was going to go to the salon Saturday morning and asked for her to come in at least by 9:00 or

10:00 a.m. so that I could leave to go by Mrs. Pierson's house to pick up the shutters and put them on our windows.

The weather was supposed to get worse as the day went on. So by 9:30 a.m. I called home to find out why she wasn't at the shop yet. She said she was on the phone paying a few bills and she would be there as soon as she was done. By 10:30 I knew I had to leave, so I told Tasha to tell anyone that came in I was gone for the day. I got the shutters and went home to put them up.

As I pulled up, our son Michael's car was there. I thought, *Good, he can help me put up the shutters.* By this time N'kosi was coming from the garage with a frown on his face, telling me that he was hungry and that Mommy wouldn't get him anything to eat. "She's been on the phone all morning," he said. I then told him I would get him something to eat but to hold on for just a few more minutes.

I walked up the stairs to our bedroom to find Connie still lying in bed, still talking on the phone. Realizing my presence, she turned away quickly, and just the feeling in the room made me feel uneasy. She soon put the phone to her chest to mute it, looked up at me, and asked, "Yes?"

The way she asked made me reply, "Is this some private conversation?"

"Yeah," she replied, which made me truly realize this was no bill-paying conversation based of the tone in her voice.

I asked, "Who is that on the phone?"

"I can talk to anyone I want to," she said.

"I never said you couldn't, but who's on the phone?" I replied.

I knew as she said, "No, hold on," that the person on the other end had asked if she wanted them to call her back. For some reason I started looking around for her cell phone. She reached down next to her, picked it up, and asked, "Are you looking for this?" and threw it to me. "You can check the numbers." I noticed that she was talking on the cordless from downstairs so I made a motion to pick up the other phone off the nightstand next to the bed. That's when Connie said to someone "I got to go, bye," hanging up so quickly the phone fell from her hand.

"Who was that on the phone?" I asked.

"Nobody," she stammered, "A friend of mine," she added.

"Which is it, nobody or a friend?" I muttered, trying to make out what she said.

Most people by now would not know what to say. But if there is one thing you need to know about Connie it is this: she did not rattle easily, and when she did, well, you knew something was wrong. The weird thing is, for the past month or so, this had been happening a lot. Especially those times when I left the salon and came home earlier than usual. Now, it was time to bring this thing—whatever it was—to a head. I reached down and picked up the phone from the floor and pushed redial. "Hey, baby, did he leave already? Now we can finish. I was about to c—"

"About to what?" I yelled into the phone. "Is that you, Kelly? What's going on here?" Dial tone. She hung up, but I knew.

"So that's it huh?" I asked. "I can't believe this…"My voice trailed off as I felt a slump in my stomach. Life as I had known it had just ended.

Up till now, I thought it was just an unfulfilled fantasy, but now everything was coming into focus. My wife was having an affair with another woman, and not just any woman but her best friend Lisa's woman Kelly. I really didn't know how or what to feel or say. Once again, I just felt numb. I stood there with a piece of paper in my trembling hands thinking that I needed to calm down. As I turned toward the bathroom to run cold water on my face, I flung the paper that I tore from the box that was sitting next to the bed toward her and kept walking .The only thing I could think of was to stay calm; that's how I am when I am angry. After I splashed my face to calm down, I came back into the room, looked at Connie, and said, "Get your stuff and get out. I will sell the house, give you half the money plus half of the money in the bank, and send you all of your clients!"

She replied, "I'm not going anywhere. I'll show you!" She walked to the door and yelled for Michael who was in his bedroom. She started yelling, "He hit me, he hit me!" Of course if you tell a son that, he's going to want to fight that person. That's exactly what happened.

Michael rushed toward me yelling, "You hit my mother!"

I raised my hand to stop him and calmly said, "I didn't hit your mom. Go back to your room; you don't know what's going on."

He got in my face but just enough to push me. I thought about Connie. She had to know that he would react that way. For some reason, Connie got between the two of us, but in a way to escalate the scene more. She wanted Michael to fight me for something she had just lied about. You could see Michael was conflicted. *Here's the man who helped raise me, but my mom said he hit her.* Even though Michael was an adult, he probably didn't know exactly what to do. He knew I loved him and I knew he loved me. So even though he was in my face, he never tried to swing at me. He was respectful like that.

At some point they went downstairs. I too went downstairs then came back up and sat on the bed. After about fifteen or twenty minutes, I heard a policeman downstairs calling my name.

Chapter 14

"MR. COOPER?" ONE OFFICER ASKED.

"Yes," I answered.

"We hear you are having a problem."

"Yes we do," I said. "You need to tell her to get up out of here."

Pause.

"Well, that's not what Mrs. Cooper is telling us. Can you come down here?"

"Sure," I said as I walked down the stairs. When I reached the bottom I still didn't know exactly why they were there until he said, "Mrs. Cooper said you hit her."

I replied, "Do you see anything on her that would suggest to you that I did anything to her? It would seem to me that if I had, you would see a mark or some pulled clothes or something."

He said to me, "That's not what your wife said."

"Well, my wife is lying," I replied.

He said, "You sit down and I will stay here with you while Officer Peter goes outside with Mrs. Cooper to see what's going on."

That officer went outside with my wife for about ten minutes and came back. I noticed he had handcuffs in his hands, and said, "Mr. Cooper, we're going to have to arrest you for domestic violence." For a second I must have blacked out because it sounded like he said he had to arrest me. Well, I hadn't, and he had said exactly that! He took the handcuffs and asked me to put my hands behind my back. I have to tell you it seemed like a dream. I was in absolute shock! They took me outside with my neighbors standing around, looking on. Embarrassment was just one of many feelings I was having. Later I would find out that most of them felt that I had done nothing. I sat in back of the police car handcuffed. You have to sit to one side slightly leaning to one side to keep from hurting your hands. I could kind of see over the top of the door to see Connie talking to the police. It would be a little later before I would learn what she was telling them. The day had taken a wrong turn, and the journey was getting worse.

On the way to the station I sat in silence. Kind of laid back looking up at the sky and a few light poles going by as the policeman said something that made me sit straight up. He leaned back and said, "Your wife is throwing everything but the kitchen sink at you." At first I thought he was talking about the domestic violence claim. But he went on to say, "Man, she's even saying you raped her."

What I said as I sat up was, "You got to be kidding me."

"Don't worry; my sergeant told me don't even think about putting that in the report unless she wants to pursue such a claim. It's obvious to us that it isn't so," he said. Before hearing this I was just mad, but now I was pissed and insulted. To think of all the women who have to be protected from abusive men *for real*, and to have her use a false claim as a tool to get me out of my house and business was as low as you can get. This really angered me. How could this be happening? She falls in love with another woman and lies to keep it a secret, then she lies to the police and *I* end up handcuffed and in the back of a police car on my way to jail. I was totally stunned. But being stunned was more comforting than being angry, so I got back to focusing on how I got there in the first place. And more importantly, how do I get out.

I was arrested and booked for domestic violence, which meant that I couldn't get bonded until I went before a magistrate. But with the hurricane coming that night, they closed the courts down until Monday morning. So I sat in jail for two of the longest nights of my life. To make matters worse, I couldn't remember anyone's phone number. That is the bad thing about cell phones; you never have to remember numbers. So

I was not only sick but also the comfort of being in touch with someone outside of jail had dried up with my memory. Then I calmed down and started to really concentrate on the last time that I called Steve. I thought about what the screen on my phone read and started to remember some of the numbers.

I walked over to the phone line, still trying to put the numbers together. I was next in line and hoping that my numbers were right. I kept repeating them over and over again in my mind. The inmate in front of me ended his call, and I stepped up, picked up the phone and slowly dialed the numbers, and waited for the connection. The phone started to ring, and someone picked up the phone and said, "Hello, Steve speaking." It was my brother-in-law, answering with the greeting that he always answered with.

I was so happy to hear his voice that everything started to come out at one time, and probably sounded jumbled up. But he understood and responded by saying, "Don't worry; we've already been up there, and I'm here at a bail bondsman's office trying to get you out."

You see, when you're in jail, it's so confined and isolated that you don't understand that things are going on outside the walls that concern you. In my case, I had friends who were doing all they could to get me out.

I said to him, "I didn't do anything to Connie."

"I know," he said. "You don't have to convince me because I know you. And not just me, but nobody else believes that you did either."

I was so relieved because it was so important to me that I wasn't looked on as someone who would hit a woman. So I said, "Thanks for believing me."

Then his voice slowed down, as if he really wanted me to understand him. "Look, they're not going to give you bail until you go in front of a magistrate, and that won't be until Monday morning."

Then he paused for my response, which was silence. All I could think of was, *Today is Saturday; I have to be here for two nights?* "That's all that can be done?" I asked.

"Yes, we've done everything. But don't worry I'll be back."

"I know you will," I said. "Where's N'kosi," I asked. "And did he see any of this?"

"No, we picked him up and he's at our house. He's worried that he won't see you again and wants to know where you are. We don't quite know what to tell him yet." Then the phone was about to turn off. So mid-sentence I stopped and said, "Tell N'kosi I said I love him and that I'm okay." And with that the phone went dead.

Now, my attention was on what next. I thought, *How in the hell am I going to sleep here for two nights?* With all that was happening and going on in my mind, I probably wouldn't get any sleep that night anyway.

As evening came, dinner was served. It was a concoction of some kind of shell pasta with what looked like bits of chicken. But I'm not sure. A slice of bread, mixed vegetables, juice, and a banana. I had the banana right out of the peeling. So I knew it was safe. After dinner, we were allowed to sit in a big open area. Some talked, some looked at television. But I could do neither. This was the time that it hit me just what had taken place today. I was trying to wrap my brain around the fact that my wife had come out of the closet as a lesbian and had been having a relationship with her best friend's partner right under her nose. And mine too, to be honest. And because of that, I was in jail. There was something wrong with this picture.

That's how my night went. One minute shocked, one minute angry. I would be lying if I said that I wasn't wishing that I had choked the hell out of her. But those were only thoughts. And if I had, then I would have felt better about being in jail because I would have deserved it. But it never took place, and that kept me up all night, wondering how many times the four of us were out to dinner and the two were playing footsies under the table. Or the few times when Kelly was at the house, even in the bedroom. Had I just missed something? How many other of our circle knew what was going on? More and more questions with no answers.

Now, I know this sounds paranoid, but sitting in jail gives you time to think of stuff like this. That's how I spent all night until morning when I heard a loud click and release, which was the door to the cell being opened for breakfast.

The only thing that I could take in for breakfast was juice. But even still I wasn't feeling so good and was sent to the infirmary. This was the first time I understood the meaning of high blood pressure, and mine was too high. They gave me blood pressure pills and sent me back to my cell. So, for the remainder of the day I mostly stayed in the cell, occasionally coming out to sit out in the rec area, not talking much. I was still pissed.

I bypassed lunch and dinner. Believe me I tried, but couldn't get it to go down. By lights out I was dehydrated and weak. By the next morning I got out of bed for breakfast but passed out on the floor. The inmates in my cell jumped up and picked me up. But instead of calling the guards, one ran and got some of the cereal and milk from one of the trays, came back and said, " Look, man, you don't want to go to the infirmary or God knows how long before you get to see a magistrate and bond out of here. Take this cereal and eat as much as you can." They took the cereal and poured the milk and sugar in and fed it to me, then water, then OJ, and soon I was feeling better. They walked me around the cell and soon they were calling us to come to court.

All shackled together, we were herded like cattle to the courtroom for a bond hearing. Mine was for domestic violence and some of the cases that came before me looked scary. I mean some bonds were fifty and sixty thousand dollars. Heck, if mine was that high, I knew I couldn't come up with that. But then I looked over and realized that Steve, my brother-in-law, was sitting in the courtroom. He looked at me and mouthed off the words, "Don't worry." That was the first sign of relief for me. The judge got to me and set my bail at one thousand dollars, which meant coming up with one hundred dollars. Steve looked up and gave me the thumbs up. After which he got up and went out the courtroom doors to go and pay my bond.

The man handcuffed to me looked over and said, "Way to go, man, you can make that."

"Yeah, thank God," I replied.

After court, we were led back to our cells for the long wait. The bail process to be released takes a long time. But I knew I was going home. Well, at least getting out. It took what seemed like forever, but soon they called my name. I turned around to thank the guys in my cell, then turned and walked out.

When I got my belongings I walked outside not knowing where to go, since they had put an automatic restraining order on me. I couldn't go home, and since Connie and I worked together, I couldn't go to work either. My whole world had just changed because of a lie. I had been locked up because of a lie that someone else told.

As I entered the lobby, I looked up and saw Steve; he was married to Connie's sister, Sandy. I can't tell you how relieved I was. Sandy had told Steve to bring me to their home. When we got in the car, I totally broke down. I guess I needed to cry, seeing that I had been keeping everything inside me all this time. You can't cry in jail, at least I don't recommend it. Steve said, "Let it out, man, you deserve to be able to let it out!" He and Sandy had already gone over to my house and brought my clothes and car over to their house. Sandy had made dinner, and even though I had no appetite, I ate and then took a shower. It was one long shower. It seemed like I couldn't get the smell of jail off of me.

After being visited by friends who were both shocked and disappointed, I had to figure out what just happened and, more importantly, what to do. I kept going back and forth over it in my mind. How could you let a woman take your wife? Was there something I could have done to prevent it from happening? Was I not man enough? That couldn't be it because no other man was involved; a woman took her! I mean, it seemed like I beat myself up so badly, questioning my own manhood. Yep, the ego was the first to go.

The fact is, it had nothing to do with me. I was married to a woman who was trying to fit into how everyone around saw her. There was a need to look successful, have a husband, kids, and house with a white picket fence. I was her *third* husband, and I've come to understand now that those marriages ended for the same reason. A woman. I think that unless I knew how to grow a vagina and tits, the overall result would have been the same.

During this time, my mind went back and forth. One minute I wanted to work it out and the next minute I didn't. At the time, I really didn't understand that it wasn't my choice. My wife was attracted to women and that was that! Even if I wanted to go back I couldn't; the restraining order made it illegal for me to be there.

Chapter 15

AFTER THE FIRST TWO DAYS, I realized that I was never going to feel comfortable staying at my in-laws home. But no sooner than I could get the thought out, that prayer was answered. A few months earlier, my brother-in-law had rented an apartment. He and his wife were going through a moment. He got uppity and had gone out and gotten an apartment, calling himself going to leave her. So, to his surprise, she helped him move. I mean she gave him the old living room furniture, pots, pans, and everything else he needed. But he only stayed there a few nights. Now he was tied into a one-year lease. Luckily for me, he was back home and he didn't want to mess up his credit by breaking the lease. "Gary, you can stay at the apartment until you can get back on your feet," he told me. He told me that I could pay him whatever rent I could afford since he had to pay the rent regardless.

I moved into the apartment with N'kosi. Thank God he was with me. It gave me a reason to stay sane. He needed me and, truth be told, I needed him too.

One morning as I was ironing Kosi's clothes to get him ready for school, I thought I was doing a good job at keeping a brave face on what I was going through, but I guess children feel your spirit. Kosi walked over to me with a Bible that a friend had given me, looked up at me holding out the book taking my hand, and said, "Daddy, read the book of Job; it will make you feel better."

I looked down at him and asked, "What did you say?"

He replied, "Let's read Job. Come read it to me."

Surprised I asked, "Where did you get that from?"

"I don't know, it just came to me," he said, shrugging his shoulder.

Well, the book of Job is about a man who lost it all, but because of his unwavering faith in God he regained everything and then some. And truth be told, we had lost everything, which made me realize I had to strengthen *my* faith. Even though that is easier said done, it helped me look at what we were going through from a more spiritual point of view, which is where I came up with the saying "finding the God in what you are going through." Simply put, the lesson is more important than the struggle.

Soon it was time to find a salon to work out of. With the automatic restraining order, I wasn't allowed to go to my shop. So getting my client list was not at all possible. Plus, I had only $216 to my name. Connie had emptied the money out of our bank account. Financially, I had to start over from scratch! I was beginning to feel like Job. I found a shop not far from my old shop that was close enough for my clients to find me, but not in a way to run into Connie. Luckily, it wasn't far from N'kosi's school, because he was having a hard time dealing with the sudden change and would get sick in school. I would have to pick him up. Sometimes I would even have to sit with him in the mornings outside the school to calm him down in order to get him ready to go inside.

It was during this time that I realized we needed therapy. I was having thoughts of suicide and N'kosi needed help to cope with all the changes, while Connie was enjoying herself with her girlfriend. Did she even care about what this was doing to our kids? It was quite obvious she didn't care about me. I remembered my father-in-law saying to me, "Toughen up, be a man!" I felt bad because I felt like I wasn't handling it like a man, until the therapist told me not to handle it like a man.

Statistics show that most men handle it by beating one or both of the women, killing them, and sometimes themselves. So she said, "I think you're handling it well." That's how I realized that my hurt came from feeling betrayed and lied to, and not the fact that my wife came out as a lesbian.

Since I didn't have much money, N'kosi's help came about when I had a conference with his teacher. His concentration and grades had suffered. After the conference, she put him in a program in school for children whose parents were going through divorce. They met twice a week. But with N'kosi it was a double whammy. He had to not only deal with divorce but having to spend time with his mother, with another woman now sleeping in bed with his mom—a spot that his dad used to occupy. On Sunday mornings, which were the only morning his mom and dad got to sleep in, he would always come and jump in between the two of us. So, sometimes it's not what you do, but how you do it. Schools should not only help with kid's therapy from divorced parents, but the transition of kids whose parents come out of the closet and divorce.

It is my belief that when you live in a world with so many types of relationships, and we don't help kids to understand that regardless of their sexuality they are worthy of someone's love and respect, the kids become confused. Maybe one day we can live in a world where people can be who they are from the start and not take other people down their road. Somewhere down that road, it's going to come down to people having to face themselves. And more than likely, other people will have to face it with them and have no say so in the matter. I hope this is not too much to expect. N'kosi went through a tough time because of his mother's total disregard of how it affected him or anybody else. And then again, I would imagine that coming out is so overwhelming, that maybe nothing else matters. So I had to really work to help him understand that this had nothing to do with his mom being a lesbian.

I had friends and long-time customers who were lesbians call me to apologize, in hopes that I wouldn't blame and dislike all lesbians for what one did. My reply was always, "I know the difference."

The road to rebuilding my life was a long but redeeming journey, and God continued to work in my life, preparing the road ahead of me.

Even the mild heart problem and diagnosis of congestive heart failure (CHF) took the focus off my divorce problems and caused me to deal with myself; therefore, I never looked back. I really needed to get back to being productive. As I said, I only had $216.00, which was the money I had made the morning I was arrested. I had to give the new shop owner $125.00 for the first week's chair rental. Then I bought a two-pack regular and two-pack supreme relaxer, a bottle of shampoo, conditioner, spirits, oil sheen, a cheap blow dryer, curling irons, a few combs, and a pair of cheap scissors.

I could find only a few of my customers, with the help of Tasha who was still at the old shop. She only got a chance to answer the phone a few times because Connie started coming in the mornings to prevent her from catching any calls for appointments for me. Connie would make the appointments for me, and when my client came, she would say that I was out but she would do their hair. Or she would tell them that I would be back soon or I was on vacation for two weeks, but she could do their hair. She gave many excuses for my absences.

Soon she asked Tasha to leave, which shocked her, but Tasha came to my shop and started over. It was a good move, seeing that she had her own customer list. This chain of events showed me how included in my journey Tasha really was. From Tasha being in a woman's group with Connie, she started to recall different discussions about lesbian issues and certain comments about the fun we were having hanging out with Kelly and Lisa, and going to different parties with them. Connie would get defensive if any perceived negative comments were made about any lesbian issues. Someone defending perceived gay and lesbian comments is not a sign of one's sexuality, I do it all the time, but in retrospect, this was one of many early indications of Connie's sexuality.

In the first week or two, not some but all of those who came paid one hundred dollars for any service they got. I don't know how or who started it, but for a simple fifteen-dollar haircut, they paid one hundred dollars and told me to keep the change. A twenty-five dollar wash and blow dry, one hundred dollars. So by the end of the week, I had made over one thousand dollars. This was enough to pay that week's chair rental and buy more supplies.

By now word had spread about what had happened, and even more, how it had happened. Again, it's not what you do, but how you do it. Most people were disgusted by the deception—Connie stabbing her two best friends, her husband, and Lisa her main ace, in the back. (Others were disgusted that it was with another woman and some who didn't know, which bothered them most.) Many people came for other reasons as well. Like to hear gossip or to just see me. It was as if my wife's coming out would make me look different or something. Then there were my customers from the islands. You see, being gay or lesbian in Jamaica can get one killed. So there came outrage from a whole different level. One woman was so upset that she was tempted to go to Connie's salon, walk in, spit on the floor, and walk out. I guess you start to understand Connie's fear of being who she saw in the mirror. But most importantly, real friends were concerned about my children, who, by this time, were trying to find normal lives. I was concerned and hoping that N'kosi wouldn't have to endure other kids picking on him about his mother. We got lucky; he didn't. But children's lives are like many others that are touched by a parent's coming out. So it goes back to, it's not what you do but how you do it.

Chapter 16

ONE DAY I WAS SITTING in the salon thinking of ways to reach more of my clients when an old friend came by the shop to see me. I hadn't seen him in a while. But he came to tell me that he understood what I was going through, because he had been through the same thing. Well, that really got my attention. I said, "Let's sit outside." Sitting outside on the window ledge, he began to tell me of the time when he was married and living in Chicago. He and his wife had what he thought was a good marriage. His wife met a girl who would become her best friend. They spent a lot of time together doing what he thought was girl talk. One day he got sick and went into the hospital. During this time he didn't see his wife as much as he thought he should, but he just figured she was working and taking care of the house, thus, didn't have a lot of time to visit. He didn't think much of it.

A friend came by to visit him at the hospital and asked, "How much have you seen your wife? I keep seeing Judy's car parked in the yard whenever I pass by the house." Even though that was in the mid-seventies, he could remember it like yesterday. He walked right out of the hospital, took a cab home, walked into the house straight into the bedroom to find his wife and her friend in bed together. I looked at him and said, "Wow, I guess I was lucky. I never had to walk in and see anything." That mental picture would have been hard to get rid of. He said, "That's why I moved here, to start over. I just needed to get away from the whispers about my manhood or lack thereof," he said. The fact that a woman took your wife from you is a hard pill to swallow for most men.

Gary Cooper

I had always thought that he was a playboy. He had that look that you would think any woman would want. He was a tall, well-built man, about 6'1", salt-and-pepper wavy hair, beard, and mustache, well groomed, always well dressed, and a real cool vibe about himself. I had no idea he was once a good faithful husband. He told me this was his first time talking about it since then. He just needed to share this with me so that I wouldn't think I was the only one who had gone through this. He then offered me his ear anytime I needed someone to listen. That would be the first of many men who would come to tell me their stories of the same.

In our little area, I guess you can say my episode was a little more public than most. I became the example of what happens when you let your wife hang out with a lesbian. Now, even though I've heard this often, nothing could be further from the truth. I have one friend who comes to mind on that subject. Her best friend is lesbian. They've been friends since high school. Nothing more, nothing less. For some reason, there are those who think that all lesbians want all women. Like it can rub off like chalk or that all gay men are looking at your booty, or want it. I have so many clients and friends who are lesbians. Their relationships are just as committed as any other, with the same problems as any others. So by no means should what happened in my marriage be considered abnormal. I can say that there are many men who are married to women who are lesbians. Some are scared; some are selfish and too uncomfortable to come out. And some too comfortable to come out. Believe me, I know some.

No more than a week had passed before another friend, who had raised a daughter, visited me. I always thought that it was good that he had raised her without her mother because I always assumed that she was dead. Not that he ever said so, but her absence seemed so final. He was so concerned about me that he shared something that was noticeably hard for him to talk to me about. He told me about his wife's friend, a girl who turned out to actually be her girlfriend. He came home one day to find all her things gone. She had left him and their daughter for that woman. He just wanted me to look at how well his life had turned out and not to give up on love. I was told not to think that all women are like that. This person shared that after going through all that pain, he had found a wife and was happily married.

I was blown away. To look at his life you would never think he went through so much. He said some nights he would cry on his daughter's shoulder and some nights she would cry on his. All he had was God and his daughter. He said that God pointed him to Florida, and that's where he rebuilt his life. In that same week, another long-time friend who shared his experience with this very same issue visited me.

His girlfriend from high school went away to college and was paired to live in the dorm with a girl who was also a freshman. Soon she was no longer just a roommate but also a friend. In the beginning, he would come to visit, and the three would go out to the movies, clubs, or just hang out together. Before too long, things started to get strange during his visits. His girlfriend began to act differently. He couldn't quite explain it in his mind, but he could feel it. The roommate who used to treat him cordially was now acting cold toward him.

One Valentine's Day, he called himself surprising his girlfriend, but neither she nor her roommate was anywhere to be found. Since she didn't call him, he started to think that she had met a guy at school and was secretly seeing him behind his back. He started to walk around the campus hoping to run into someone who may have seen her. But instead, he ran into her and her roommate getting off the bus. While approaching them, he got the feeling that he wasn't supposed to run into them. He said he asked them what was going on. His girlfriend's roommate seemed angry and walked away and said under her breath, "You tell him." That was when she came clean and said she didn't mean for it to happen, but the two had started a relationship that had gone further than friendship. She admitted that she always felt "that way" but didn't realize for certain if it was truly who she was. But now she knew for sure. She didn't know how she felt it could fit into her life, until now. He said it felt as if the world stood still for a moment and he didn't know what to feel. He said she kept apologizing. Unfortunately for him, he too said that night has remained in his mind all these years and has affected his life to this day. I asked if he had ever had counseling to deal with his feelings. He looked at me and said, "Up until now, I was too ashamed to even talk about it."

I said to him, "Ashamed? You should not feel ashamed for other people's discoveries about themselves. It had nothing to do with you not being man enough."

Never had one issue impacted my life so much as that of women with families coming out. It's one of those things that regardless of how much of a man you are or how good a husband you may think you are, in the blink of an eye one thing can happen that will make a woman who feels that way inside have to confront herself and who she is. Because all the women that I spoke to came to that conclusion and said that even though it was forever in their mind, there was always a defining moment that changed everything. I think that moment for my wife was Gay Pride Week in New York.

Soon my eyes started to notice things that I never noticed before. I had no idea that I never noticed customers in my shop who were partners and not just friends. One day in particular in a restaurant, when my son, his girlfriend, and I were leaving, we passed a guy and his girlfriend holding hands. I spoke to them and kept on walking. My son Maurice said, "They're everywhere!" I didn't realize what he was talking about until I looked back and realized that the guy with the girl was really another woman. But she dressed, acted, and looked like a man.

That is one of the questions I'm always asked. Why would a woman leave a man to be with a woman who tries to act and look like a man? My answer is, "I have no idea." Maybe it's because of the need to show her masculine side, or could it have something to do with chromosome markers? I'm not a researcher on this matter, but much research has been done. Depending on who did the study, you seem to get different theories, some clinical, some religious, and some physical.

A great example of a woman who consciously chose to have relationships with other women instead of men is a girl I met back in the late seventies. The decision came at a very early stage in her life. Her parents were interracial. Her mother was white, her father black. Her father abandoned her and her mom. This impacted her life and forced her mom to work two jobs, which left her little time to raise her daughter.

Soon they fell on hard times and with nowhere else to go, they went to live with her mother's mom and dad, her grandparents. They were rather prejudiced and had not wanted her mother to be with a black man from the start. Living at her grandparents' house was always uncomfortable. When she was around age twelve or thirteen her grandfather and uncles would rape her. She would tell me, "I guess they were curious about what it felt like to have sex with a black woman." She felt she couldn't tell her mother because, as most kids do, she thought she was the reason for their misfortune. But on the other hand, the mother should have protected her from this. So this put a strain on her relationship with her mom.

She graduated from high school and went away to college. In college she met a guy she thought she could trust as a friend. One night they were going to the movies. When he picked her up, he said he left something in his room and needed to go back to get it. They got to the dorm and he asked her to come with him instead of staying in the car, because it was dark. When she got up to the room, he said, "You can sit on the bed." She didn't think much about it, at first. Next thing she knew he was on top of her. She said it was like having an out-of-body experience. She realized that all she could do was lay there and stare up at the ceiling. When it was over she couldn't say anything. She put her clothes back on and left. He started trying to apologize then turned it into, "Since you didn't stop me, I thought you wanted it." He had no idea just how deep this went.

So after that she swore off men. As a matter of fact, the thought of a man disgusted her. She had made a conscious decision not to be with men anymore. And that's when her mind became open to being with a woman. One of two things happened. Either that was the defining moment that had her seeing what she already was, or that every man in her life had been a piece of crap and she didn't think that there were any men who ever meant her any good.

Chapter 17

THEN THERE'S THE CLINICAL RESEARCH that studies chromosomes, and there are many conclusions on that too. According to an article written by Mitch King,[1] there is statistical evidence that one form of male homosexuality is genetically transmitted from mothers to their sons through the X chromosome. Could the same be true for women who are lesbians? The above article cited research done in 1993 by Dean Hamer and colleagues at the National Institutes of Health. The research claimed to have discovered a gene for homosexuality.

Their study used a sample of forty "gay" brother pairs whose sexual orientation was said to be maternally inherited. About 83 percent of the pairs shared the same markers on a region of the X chromosome called Xq28. However, in 1999, in the largest study of its kind up to that date, Rice, Ebers, and colleagues at the University of Western Ontario failed to reproduce a statistically significant linkage to the Xq28 marker in a sample of fifty-two gay brother pairs. Further evidence of a genetic link to homosexuality has not been produced. But nonetheless, most scientific organizations believe that being gay or lesbian is not a choice, that biology plays some role.

The National Mental Health Association says most researchers believe sexual orientation is complex and that biology plays an important role, which means that many people are born with their sexual orientation or

1. Mitch King, 1995, article "Homosexuality: It's in Your Genes (Not Just Your Jeans), accessed September 21, 2016, http://www.qrd.org/qrd/origins/1995/homosexuality.is.in.your.genes-06.27.95

that it's established at an early age. As you may see, it all depends on who is doing the research.

Does it matter whether homosexuality is a choice or if it's something one is born with? Shouldn't gay and lesbian people be afforded the same rights as heterosexuals whether being gay or lesbian is a choice or not? I would think that being a human being is enough. Then there's the religious point of view that divides families over this matter.

Imagine mothers and fathers who totally cut off their parental relationships with the child who God brought into the world through them. And this is the beginning of the fake relationships leading to marriages to men who never stood a chance from the start of the relationship. This brings it back to me.

I was starting to get closure for the day of having to defend myself in court for domestic violence that never took place. Even though the problem I faced was all about male energy other than my own, I was still treated like a man. She was still treated like a woman. Even though there was not one scratch, one tear of clothes, or any other sign that I did anything, I was still treated like a man who had committed domestic violence.

One day Linda, a friend of Connie's and mine, said, "Gary, I happen to know that you didn't do anything to Connie, and I'd be willing to testify on your behalf." When asked to explain, she said, "On the day they took you to jail, I was shocked and went to the house to find out what happened. I asked Connie if you hit her." She said Connie looked at her and said, "No, he didn't hit me. I just needed to get the negative out of the house and business. But don't worry, I'll undo it and make it right." Her undoing it was to not press charges. But the state picked it up anyway and the case continued. Connie had a choice: tell them I lied, that it never happened, or stick with the lie. She chose to stick with the lie.

Chapter 18

I CALLED THIS TIME THE sorting out period. You see, a lot of things were happening at the same time, but all came together at once. First, an old customer who was an attorney heard that I needed an attorney, but money was tight. She took my case pro bono because she just knew I didn't do it and knew that I both needed and deserved justice.

The second thing was the annuity that Connie and I had for our retirement. Connie got a surrender form, forged my name, got someone to notarize the document, sent it to the holder, got the check, and forged my name again. She deposited it in our joint account that was left open with about $5.00, and then transferred the funds to her account. When I went to the police I'm pretty sure if I had done what she did I would be sitting in jail. Instead, I was told to just talk to her and try to get it back. What an irony! The last time I checked, forgery was against the law.

If it had gone to trial when I wanted to, I would still be waiting for my money. So on the first day, which was jury selection, my attorney showed the prosecutor copies of the forged document, cancelled check, deposit and transfer forms. My lawyer said to the prosecutor, "Now that you are prosecuting my client for that, you have to prosecute her for this, right?" As the prosecutor looked at the documents, he never said a word. He just walked over to the table where Connie sat and put the documents on the table in front of her. I couldn't hear, but the shocked look on her face showed everything. Not only didn't she know that I knew about it but that I had copies of the forged documents. I watched her fumble through the papers trying to think of something to say. I saw the prosecutor say something to her and come back over to our table. He said to us, "I told her to have a cashier's check for half the amount and bring it to court tomorrow."

After jury selection, I told Tasha what happened. She smiled and said to me, "I told you everything's going to work out." It was moments like these that got me through this entire experience. I could see God's reason for putting her in my life. I had all this feminine energy surrounding me—mostly females surrounded me, praying for me, nurturing me, holding me up. These were the angels that God sent to cover me. And there's nothing like having women on your side, especially if you're a man dealing with problems that are female in nature. But it goes past gender.

On the morning of the trial, I sat nervously in the courtroom, not knowing if the jury had the ability to believe a man over a woman on a domestic violence charge. The prosecution had already come to that conclusion without even hearing one word from me. They tried to settle before court by offering me six months' probation and anger management. I looked at them and said, "No way!"

Their reply was, "Mr. Cooper, if found guilty you can spend up to one year in jail."

I responded, "I can live with going on the stand telling the truth, and them not believing me. But I can't live with admitting to something I didn't do, and I told you I didn't do it." The prosecutor walked back over to the table where Connie was sitting and took the cashier's check from her. He brought it over and gave it to me. I guess that was a sign of how the trial was going to go.

The trial started with both attorneys making opening statements. Then testimony from Connie followed by our older son, who had no clue as to what happened, let alone why he was there. Next the arresting officer gave his testimony. But the most memorable moment for me was the first officer's cross-examination by my attorney. His testimony was, when he got there he found the room in disarray. She asked him to explain disarray. He replied, "Well, there was clothing all over the room, shoes over the floor, boxes everywhere."

She asked, "Did you notice anything else that was going on in the room?"

He thought for a minute, then replied, "No."

She said, "Are you sure?"

He thought again and replied, "Not that I can remember."

So she said, "Did you notice wood or anything in the room?"

"No," he said.

"Well, if you had noticed, the reason the clothes, shoes, and boxes were in the room was because he was laying a wood floor and was now doing the closet. So, to do that he had to take everything out of the closet. And all the things you saw in the room were from the closet."

But he never noticed. He just never investigated any further than first impressions. Had he looked further, he would have also noticed a saw and other tools.

Finally it was my attorney's turn to put on our defense. She put me on the stand and I testified. When I began to testify, I think the story started to sound different to the jury than the prosecutor's opening statement. Then I was cross-examined. To which the prosecutor tried to use tricks like asking me my answer in different ways. But regardless of how many ways you ask a question, the truth in the answer will always be the same.

Tasha was called to the stand, then Linda; they both went through the same process as I did. Next were the closing arguments. I kid you not when I say part of the prosecutor's closing words for domestic violence was that I flung a piece of paper. It's amazing how much better you feel when your attorney's closing argument is flowing with truth!

With that, the judge gave the jury instructions and then let them go into the jury room to reach a verdict. As I walked through the courtroom doors, I was about to say to Tasha and my attorney, "Let's go get some coffee," but before I could get the words out, the bailiff stuck his head out the door and yelled, "They have a verdict." We looked at each other surprised. It only took what seemed like about five or ten minutes. We all returned to the courtroom, and the courtroom door closed. The bailiff had us all rise and brought out the judge. After which, he brought in the jury. The judge asked, "Do you have a verdict?"

"Yes," the foreman answered.

The bailiff took the verdict from the foreman and gave it to the judge. He read it and gave it to a woman who would then read the verdict aloud. My attorney and I anxiously stood to hear it.

I can't even begin to tell you how I was feeling. But they say that just before you die your whole life flashes before your eyes. Well, I believe the same also happens just before a verdict is read. Your life flashes before your eyes. The entire time I was thinking, *How in the hell did I get to this point?* I looked at the lips of the person who was about to say the words that would dictate the next year of my life. As the verdict was read, it came out in a blur. But the two words that came out clearly to me were, "NOT GUILTY." For the first few seconds, I couldn't move. It was like I just went blank. Then I looked up and said, "Thank you, God!" Next I looked at the jury who were all looking at me smiling, and I mouthed the words, "Thank you so much."

I then looked over to my attorney, hugged her, and thanked her for believing me. Then I looked back at Tasha and gave the thumbs up. I don't recall exactly how the judge dismissed the court because I was imagining the judge saying, "Let the court say amen." After most had left the room, the judge looked over at the prosecutor and said, "Some cases should never come to trial, and this was one of them." The prosecutor came over and shook our hands and said, "Good luck." So, to me, it seemed like it was nothing personal. He was simply doing his job.

My wife slithered out of the courtroom right after the verdict. One would think that after all this, she would just be fair in dissolving our marriage and splitting our possessions. Wrong. This was only the beginning.

The next day I dropped our son off to school and went to the shop. But when it was time to pick him up, he wasn't there. I waited, walked back and forth to the school, up and down the street worrying. I always picked him up at the crossing walk of the school.

In the midst of my panicking, my cell phone rang. It was Connie calling to tell me she had picked N'kosi up from school. Relieved, I said, "Okay," and hung up the phone. The next day when I got to the shop Tasha had put together a small party to congratulate me on the verdict. She had gone to the trouble of getting my friends and customers to take time out of their day to come. I felt so happy and honored that I had to go to the back of the building to cry. My friend Val came to the back and gave me an old-fashioned mama-grandmother hug. This had such a calming effect on me. It made me feel as though everything would be all right.

But all of the good feelings were brought to a sudden halt when a sheriff walked into the shop. He was looking for Gary Cooper. Puzzled I said, "I am he." He was there to serve me with a restraining order from Connie. I took the order from him and read it. I was surprised by the part that suggested that Connie was fearful for her life. I was ordered to stay five hundred feet from Connie, my child, and his school, and that a copy was also served to the school. I was no longer calm. My attorney, who was also there, took the papers from my hand and started to read them. The officer first asked her to leave until she identified herself as my attorney. She asked him a few legal questions, then said, "Don't worry. I will be at the courthouse first thing in the morning to get this resolved." I had never called my wife, never passed the shop or the house since the day I was arrested. As a matter of fact, the last time I had even seen the house or salon was the day that I was arrested. She thanked the officer and he left. She told me, "Let's finish celebrating." I must admit, the mood had changed at the shop, but not too much. I was just amazed at how many people cared. God is good.

Gary Cooper

The next day, my attorney called me from the courthouse to let me know she was able to get an emergency hearing for custody. I had no idea why Connie did this, because before my verdict, she didn't even want to be bothered with N'kosi. So I could only assume that this was a move to try to keep the house, because being a woman crying crocodile tears and lying was no longer enough to win in court. We used to always laugh and joke about a woman getting her way in a divorce by crying and lying.

So, on the first hearing, we were given a temporary schedule, which jumped N'kosi back and forth like a piece in a checkers game. He would get dropped to school Monday. I would pick him up and drop him off to school Tuesday. Connie would pick him up Tuesday and drop him off Wednesday, and so forth. Then we would alternate weekends. All of this because she wanted to be with another woman, wow!

Kosi felt like a wind-up toy and was getting to the point where he was beginning to resent his mother. In so many words, he even went so far as to tell me his mother getting killed would be the answer to his problem. He just hated to go to his mother's because within a few months she had moved another woman into the house and did not consider how he felt or what was the proper way to introduce him to her new lifestyle or her new mate. It all came at once.

So it continued to affect his behavior and grades in school. Kosi wasn't the only casualty of Connie's way of doing things. Michael was starting to get the real picture of what had taken place and that he had been lied to. I know it had to bother him. Because of a bunch of lies, he almost had a fight with me, the man who was truly a father to him. Connie's selfish wants and desires had affected so many people in such a negative way, and she didn't seem to care.

Since Connie had moved her new woman into the house, it had become very strange for Michael to live there. His mother's new girlfriend had come in as if she had been a part owner of the house. Even he had made sacrifices in the past so that we could buy that house. All of the days after school when he would come help out at the shop shampooing heads, cleaning, washing towels, helping me build both shops, helping out at our hair and fashion shows. So, by now I guess he felt like he had invested his sweat and blood as well, so why would his mother allow this woman to come in and live in it like it was hers?

Seeing this woman come and take over the house and to see his mother transform into this other person was very disappointing and difficult for him. His mom had cut her hair into a very low cut and was coloring it a new color each week. Pink one week and red the next. She started wearing pants and skirts that came about a half inch above the lips of her vagina and openly displayed sexual intentions with her partner. So with the atmosphere at the house changing, it became too hard to stay, and he moved out. Once again, his relationship with his mother became strained. Thank God for the relationship between him and my son Koran. They were closer than brothers. Through Koran, I was able to keep an eye on Michael.

Now out on his own for the first time in his life, it would be good to say it was time for him to leave home, to become independent. But under these circumstances the result is unlikely independence, but more like resentment, disappointment, disrespect, and internal conflict brewing inside. When it's like that it may come out in different ways, producing a child who may harbor hatred for his mother and likely carry it over to the way he treats other women.

One of the many motions handed down in court was my attorney's suggestion for a court-appointed guardian ad litem to be Kosi's voice in court, but not a full voice. If it were up to him, he would be with me seven days a week. Connie's thinking was to have Kosi and get the house until he was eighteen (that would be ten years later) then sell the house and split the money from the sale. That did not happen due to the guardian ad litem who made it known up front that Kosi had no attachment to the house. We left court with the judge giving us joint custody and joint primary residence with no child support issues. Just everything down the middle: insurance, medical bills, clothing, food, education, and love and attention. The change of custody schedule made it easier for Kosi since he hated going to his mom's house anyway. At least the time there seemed shorter.

Our life began to become calmer. Most of my clients had found my location. Money had become less of an issue. Even though it was temporary, a girl had come into my life to help me feel that I still had "it." Everybody who enters your life has a place in it. The Bible says everything happens for a reason. I guess God looked down on me and felt I needed my confidence restored. So in came someone to help me understand that the universe produced more than one woman, and that in any case, a woman was not my sole purpose for living.

I was starting to see that God's purpose for my life was bigger than a house, a business, or even a woman. I was just starting to understand my strengths, my weaknesses, friends, and enemies. No matter how bad we think it can get, if we keep our minds and eyes open and put God first, we'll start to see all the great lessons and opportunities unfold before us. My life was stripped bare. I mean, I had no money because my wife had gone to the bank and taken out all we had. I couldn't go to my house or even the salon. The restraining order prevented these things. This was my "Job" moment. I had no clients because all of their contact information was in the computer at the other salon. But most found me later anyway. Some who weren't even my customers still wouldn't go back to Connie's shop. Not because my wife was a lesbian but because of the way she came out, with no regard for anyone but herself.

I guess that's my main point. There are a number of lesbians and gays in America. I think, to most people, it's no big deal anymore. But to many folks in America their religious leaders have shaped their minds to believe that people having a different sexual orientation makes them less worthy of God's love; therefore, mistreating them is okay. Even though the Bible says love your neighbor as you do yourself.

Religious leaders will say that somehow gays and lesbians are affecting our marriages and families. The way I see it is that when we judge people for who they feel they are or how they feel inside, we help create a world where a woman will become afraid and try to fit into the role that society dictates. Therefore, she may have a boyfriend, get married, have children and fit into a completely heterosexual lifestyle. But her desire to be with another woman will slowly come to the surface and maybe she'll go half a lifetime pushing those feelings back inside.

I think at some point it becomes harder to fit into someone else's view of oneself. I remember, at times, my wife would seem depressed and disconnected even though things were going well in our lives.

People are always asking me if there were any signs of my wife's sexual orientation. Did I see anything that would have given me a clue? The answer is both yes and no. As a man you see women as just that, women. A woman hanging out with your wife as a girlfriend, out doing so-called girlie things like shopping and going out to eat together, you never imagine her as a woman who sees your wife as you do.

Meanwhile, a relationship is developing. See, if a man were hanging out with your wife too much, you'd put a stop to it quickly because you know a man's intentions. But with a woman you never see it coming.

In the two times that our life faced this issue, one of the small things that I noticed was my wife was on the telephone constantly, even though she wasn't a person who ordinarily would spend a lot of time having long conversations with her female friends. Her demeanor while on the phone changed. There was a lot of giggling and secret chatter. After she got off the phone she would want to have sex. Her dress became more provocative. She went out and got her navel pierced, even though she wasn't into piercing. Her private area, which was shaved into what I call a landing strip, was suddenly bald. I wasn't doing anything differently, but she became alive with energy, sexually speaking, that is.

She started to seriously joke about bringing another woman into the bedroom, but I got the feeling that if I had responded differently we would have. Not for me, but for her, as a way to be with a woman and have my approval. I'm pretty sure that, in no time flat, I would have become a prop, or bystander. Let's face it, your wife knows what it's like to have sex with you, so the new experience would be with a woman.

But other things I noticed would be the same things you would see in any other deceptive relationship: not answering her phone, gone for periods of time with no real explanation, and at times getting caught in lies about her whereabouts, phone ringing and not answering it even in the middle of the night, if the phone rang and I answered it no one was there, or her deleting calls and text messages. You know, the usual cheating signs. At first I thought she was just going through a phase. I mean, after all, it was my wife, and I never saw it as anything but a phase.

People think that the women who are lesbian are more butch with big arms and muscles, tattoos everywhere, with short hair trying to be masculine like a man. But in my experiences, just like men who are gay, women come in many forms. Some are fems and some are butch (more masculine) and some are in between. Just as heterosexual men and women come in various types as well. I think we just notice it more in gays and lesbians. If I had processed it in my mind like that, then yes, I would have understood what was happening. For every man who told me his story, his experience was the same. Maybe it was the fact that my wife pursued me, not the other way around. She asked me to marry her; I didn't do the asking. She told me that she got a reading and it said we should have a child. I had never even thought of having another child.

Those things plus all the other things we did leading up to the start of our relationship, such as curling up on the sofa while eating strawberries dipped in sugar, and the many "Just because I love you" cards with some of the most loving words written by Connie.

She loved shopping, especially for shoes. Connie took great care of herself and was very feminine. Special care was given to her makeup and skin care. She put together a women's group to discuss female concerns. Connie loved and introduced me to Luther Vandross songs, and she would even do and say things that some would consider not so good about lesbians. Example: There was a time that Connie, Tasha, and I were invited to a friend's birthday party who happened to be lesbian, with most of the guests except us being the same. She wouldn't go without us and stuck by us like glue, as if it would rub off on her or some woman was going to push up on her.

So with all these things together, why would I think any different? Right now, many men are married to women who are closet lesbians. And their husbands, like me, don't have a clue. There is nothing that they can see that would make them see their wives as lesbian.

Everyone is talking about men on the "down low," but not about the women on the "down low." Most of the books and television talk shows that I've seen are usually about women whose husbands came out. The shows are usually about what the women go through. And even when the subject is a woman coming out to her husband, the show is always about what the wife went through. How she felt or how she got through it all and survived. But no one talks about what the man went through or how he felt. Now, I'm not saying that there are no such shows. It is just that I've never seen one.

I know that having a lesbian encounter or even being curious doesn't make you a lesbian, and sometimes I guess the line between the two can become blurred. I was doing a long-time client's hair one day. She was getting her hair done because it was her wedding anniversary. She touched my hand and said to me, "If it will make you feel better, I tried the lesbian thing, but it wasn't what I thought it would be. Now I've been married for thirteen wonderful years." It turns out that she was one of those curious ones. She assumed my ex was just curious too. In her opinion, Connie would realize that her actions were due to her curiosity and just wanting to experiment. That may or may not be true. And at this point, it really doesn't matter.

Would the world be a better place if all lesbians were out of the closet? Probably not! In all honesty, this is not a realistic statement. But at least women would not have to take an entire family down that road, for fear of being harmed or looked down on by their family and friends.

Gary Cooper

I think that if a woman is in the closet, she should stay there and remain single until she has the courage to come out and be who she really is. My concern is the lives of men with lesbian wives whose marriages never stood a chance from the start.

If a woman comes to terms with her sexuality, realizes that it's a woman who she wants to be with, but she is married to a man and has kids, then I think she has to consider that she is not the only one who will be affected by her coming out.

If your thinking is that you have been keeping this in all your life so you're going to just be yourself, that would make you selfish. This selfishness has nothing to do with being lesbian. Just have basic honesty and concern for the family members who are left scratching their heads. I'm no mental health professional, but I think the best way to start is to first sit down with your husband and tell him the truth. He may be shocked at first, but at the end of the day, he'll appreciate the fact that you trusted him enough to talk to him, rather than him finding out in the street or by surprise that you've been sneaking around and are already involved in a relationship with another woman. Couples should seek counseling from someone who has studied human behavior and understands the process of coming out. No offense, but I don't suggest a minister because more than likely, he'll use his or her own interpretation of the Bible to show why it is wrong. This will only cause confusion and guilt about the way she feels, and why.

I guess after going through that process, a divorce would be the next issue. If you are dealing with two people and both are trying to be fair and want to do what is best for the children, then mediation will go faster and smoother. I think dividing money, property, custody, and all the things you've built together will eliminate that part of the conflict that tends to bring about guilt. During this time, it is also important for you to deal with yourself and pursue your new life.

I would suggest seeing a psychiatric and/or a clinical professional. A good place to start will probably be one of the Gay and Lesbian

Community Centers (GLCC) in your city. More than likely they could help with all the challenges that you and your spouse will face trying to help the kids get their lives back to as normal as possible. Additionally, kids may need assistance in handling the possibility of other kids harassing or demeaning them due to choices made by their parents. Let's face it, society has not done a good job of teaching kids that there are other kinds of loving families and people different than their own, and they should be treated just like they want to be treated.

Now, coming out this way works only if you are a person who is concerned about how your actions affect people other than yourself. This process of coming out would work for someone with integrity.

Then there is the other way that I personally experienced, and the men I spoke with, had to deal with. We dealt with women who were leading double lives. Those who want the best of both worlds by having the safe family at home, while deceiving their husbands into believing that her girlfriend is just her "friend." Even when all is revealed, it's made to seem as if the man did something wrong to make it easier for the woman to face the world with her deception.

My ex-wife tried to use the laws that protect women who really do have abusive husbands for her own gain and tried to make me think that the absence of intimacy in the marriage had something to do with *my* inadequacy rather than her need for something that no *man* could ever give her. The problem with this is that a lot of men take it as a terrible blow to the male ego. It sometimes can lead to violence toward that woman, her partner, or both, and sometimes even her murder followed by his or her suicide.

Chapter 19

ANOTHER QUESTION I'M OFTEN ASKED all the time is, "Do you think you were hurt more because it was a woman?" Or "Would you be less hurt if it had been another man?" For a long time I couldn't answer either question. But now I understand that hurt is hurt. I'm just a man, and I can only process things as a man. But thank God I was put into a great position. Being a hairstylist, women surrounded me, and most of my friends are females. It is safe to say their words and nurturing helped restore my confidence. I thank God for them. So, I was able to give my situation perspective. Not all men have that kind of support system. Most that I spoke to had to deal with their buddies' insinuations and backhanded jokes. It must affect some men in a great way. Even though it was between the 70s and 90s, two of the men I interviewed picked up and moved to another state in an attempt to get away from facing anyone who knew what happened to their marriages. It took hearing about what I was going through for these men to even begin to talk about their experience, and I think they needed to finally talk about it; and I guess I really needed to listen. I will never forget the look on one of their faces when he said, "Man, that experience has got me messed up, even today." His eyes stared off as if he was reliving those moments in his mind all over again.

Being realistic, I would think a woman at this point would probably want to experiment to first see if this is what she really is or wants. Most likely, the woman is thinking that her husband couldn't handle the fact that she wants to get intimate with another woman. Even if only just to see how it will feel. To be honest, I doubt if most men could handle it. I know I couldn't. So most likely, experimentation will take place without the husband's knowledge. Based on those I've interviewed, the person you have known and hung out with may have introduced your woman to the lifestyle. At first glance, the man may notice that the two are spending time talking on the phone and going out together, even though he knows the two have nothing in common. He still might not understand what is going on.

Some women I spoke to say they knew their sexuality at a young age. So I find it very hard to believe that a woman could be in her thirties and forties without knowing. I would imagine having someone within "eye shot" is safe. Hearing my wife constantly talking on the phone and always doing that "giggle" is what happened to me. There was no way I could know what was being said on the other end of the phone line. I didn't know the giggling was really her blushing out loud and that she was responding to flirting from the other end of the phone. Soon she was walking around acting like a teenager. We started spending more time hanging out with those who I used to affectionately call, "The Lesbian Mafia." It was like a wolf pack centered around one couple, Kelly and Lisa. But they were there for each other. Almost every night was spent doing something like going to clubs, dinner, house parties, or just sitting around playing cards.

My wife became consumed with hanging out, even if I wasn't coming along anymore. Eventually, I started to realize that we were going out so much that we were always getting a babysitter to look after our son. Most of our activity wasn't really for kids.

Things were really beginning to change. I would come home at night and Connie was always at Lisa and Kelly's house. The strangest thing would happen when she would return home. She would always want sex, and I mean adventurous sex. Sometimes we would have four or five orgasms. Or she would get on the phone talking and giggling, then would get off and would be very horny. Then we would have more sex. She became more daring and wanted to do all kinds of different things in our bed. Don't get it twisted. As a man, I loved that part. As a husband wanting to please his wife, I would go to the Penthouse adult store to buy things to make our sex life more daring and adventurous. I didn't understand that another woman could only satisfy what she was searching for. These were only substitutes for her real desires. Even in New York at Gay Pride Week, when we would return to the hotel she would want to have sex, even though we were sharing a room with Kelly and Lisa. It was like she had come alive. Gone from a woman who had very little to say, to a woman with everything to say. She used to always say sex was overrated. Now she couldn't get enough!

During this time for me, being a married man was very contradicting. Our sex life before was kind of routine. A thing that married people did every now and then. But now our life was like hot sauce on collard greens. It gives greens a hell of a kick, but burns like hell coming out later. But it didn't stop there. Next she started dressing differently. Her dress slowly became more provocative and revealing. I guess almost like advertisement. By now some of the women at some lesbian parties were looking at her like a piece of meat. It was as if she was sending out a message that was saying, "I'm available." Now, in reflecting, I see this but at the time I was in denial. I doubt that I could have changed anything. By now I guess her mind was made up, "I'm coming out!"

So, when I noticed some of the women showing interest, I thought it was only from their view. I didn't understand that my wife was speaking to them by her actions, loudly and clearly. The funny thing is that when the shit hit the fan, my first thought was Kelly was going after my wife. I had to get hit in the head with a reality stick to realize that my wife had just as big a hand in what was going on as well.

Men who have gone through this wonder at some point if they hurt because it was a woman, or if they'd feel any different if it had been a man. But like I said before, hurt is hurt. But I think if in this hurt you feel the need to seek a professional, then therapy should include whatever it takes to help them understand it has very little to do with them, and more to do with their wife or girlfriend coming to terms with who she is. It doesn't make him less of a man. If a man is not much of a man, it has nothing to do with his woman being lesbian. Then I think his therapy should include understanding what was lacking in his life that failed to bring him into manhood.

Thank God everyone helped me to understand this. When we started the divorce proceedings, I approached it from the same point. The court cared less about my wife being a lesbian and at no time did I make it an issue. However, my wife tried to use this as a way to get legal support. I think she got an attorney through one of the gay-lesbian organizations. They must have thought the divorce had something to do with me being antilesbian because of the way her attorney acted toward me. Normally, attorneys are never personal. But whenever she got a chance she would bring up the fact that someone in the court system was gay or lesbian in a way that I could hear. As if to tell me, we are everywhere. I mean, this felt personal. It never dawned on her that the word *lesbian* never came out of either my mouth or my attorney's. That's because to me, it wasn't about that. It could have been another man, and to me, it would still be about betrayal.

The judge ordered mediation first, to see if a settlement could be agreed upon without a trial. So we scheduled our first meeting. I figured the only thing to settle was the house and bills since we could call the business even. She had the shop with the chairs and sinks, and I got the customers. So I said, "Let's call it even." The offer I got from her was fifty thousand dollars, and she'll pay off the debt. My reply was, "Are you crazy? Or better yet, do you think I'm crazy?" Her thinking was to make me believe the house was worth $300,000, when in fact, it was worth well over $400,000.

By our next meeting, I had gotten an appraisal, which confirmed what I believed the value of the house to be. We were able to come to an agreement of a buy-out, which allowed her to keep the house, pay off our collective debt, and buy me out of the house. She agreed to sixty days to refinance the house to get this behind us.

The paperwork was drawn up and signed. I remember leaving mediation feeling renewed. Like this would all be behind me in sixty days. I exited the building and just stood there looking up at the birds. I realized how clear the sky was and just closed my eyes. Just the feel of the sun on my face and the slight breeze made me realize the presence of God in my life.

The other side of that realization was, for as much as I realized God was in my life, Satan was still around too. As sixty days came and went, it became obvious this episode was far from over. Every lesson I learned from this experience would be put to the test. Patience, trust, love, confidence, forgiveness, and faith were all given a run for their money. Soon ninety days had passed. Then six months, and eventually a year had passed! By now, it had become clear to me she had no intention of honoring our settlement. At this point, I was trying to trust my attorney to get a court date and get back in court to enforce the court order. But I had to be patient with the slow court system. That's just the way it is. I now had very little confidence in the court system, but a lot of faith in God.

Unlike so many men who have gone through finding out their wife's real sexuality, I came through this experience with less baggage than I began with. And even though I went through a period of self-doubt, I feel more of a man because of that experience than I ever felt in my entire life.

When I reflect on what happened, I now find so much of it funny. I went through a stage that I called, "The New Car." You never notice a particular car until you buy it. Then you see the car everywhere. It wasn't until this issue affected me that I began to notice how many lesbian couples were clients of mine or were at the shop. Everywhere I went there were lesbian couples that I had never paid any attention to. I guess I just saw people as people. I would see some lesbian couples with kids and would wonder if they had left a man somewhere torn to pieces. Or if they had come out in a way that considered how this would affect those whose lives were attached to theirs.

It is estimatedere are over 41,000 same-sex couples living in Florida, and about 51 percent of them are female based on information from the 2000 census information on gay and lesbian couples[2]. About 20 percent of gay females have children under the age of eighteen living at home with them, also 27 percent of gay females state they conceived their children as part of their relationship[3]. The demographics of sexual orientation vary significantly, and estimates for the LGBT population are subject to controversy and ensuing debates. The most common ranges given for the LGBT population are from 1% to 10%according to Wikipedia[4]. This is based on those willing to admit their sexuality.

There are probably just as many still in heterosexual relationships or are married to men and are still living a life of deception. More than likely, like me, those men will never know until it comes out by accident. To them I would say, "Consider some of the signs that I saw but didn't understand. But be mindful of the one's that I didn't see at all." If it turns out that she is lesbian, some woman will come after her. As one of my more "lady butch" friends told me, "There's nothing like helping a woman over that line. Fact is you can never compete with another woman." Especially if your wife is a willing participant.

As the years started to pass, I soon started to fill in the missing pieces to my wife's explanation of her prior two marriages. They, too, had met the same demise. Always another woman. Her first husband had even

---

2. http://www.thetaskforce.org/static_html/downloads/reports/reports/2000Census.pdf
   Page: 54

3. http://www.thetaskforce.org/static_html/downloads/reports/reports/2000Census.pdf
   Page: 10

4. https://en.wikipedia.org/wiki/Demographics_of_sexual_orientation

taken her up on her offer of bringing another woman or two into the bedroom, which you would think would be every man's dream. I think in time he realized that his wife was having way too much fun.

So, soon he was just a prop. But by now it was too late and had started to become a problem in the marriage. This seems to be a pattern in her early days before me—to be in a relationship with a man for show, and sneak around with women in the shadow. Shadow dancing. Even in our marriage, only now would I find out just how far the relationship with Ruby had gone. They, too, had been intimate, which by now is funnier to me than hurtful. I guess I healed too much.

Yes, it will be painful just like any other break up, but there's light at the end of the tunnel. I am proof of that, having found the God in what I went through. It helped me to appreciate who I am, what I think, and most importantly, what I feel. This was all a part of my journey.

My child went through some whippings at his mom's house by her partner. The Child Protection Services called the whippings abusive, so for a while, he was with me and couldn't visit his mom's house. And even then, I was her biggest defender when contacted by Child Protection Services. To be honest, I hope my son's relationship with his mom works out at some point. But since he was eight, he has been living with me and only recently started having much contact with his mom. I just think that so much was thrown at him at one time. He never was that bonded to his mom because of her inability to be a nurturer. This is not to say that a woman who identifies herself as lesbian cannot be a nurturing mom. I'm just saying because of her upbringing Connie was not one. But he still deserves to have a good mother-son relationship with the woman who brought him into this world.

Kosi went to therapy and I'm looking forward to him seeing the resolution of this issue. He'll have enough to deal with in life just growing up in this world. The way he feels about his mother shouldn't be one of those issues.

Gary Cooper

My many friends have truly been part of my multiple blessings. To see who loves me and to hear how they feel about me while I'm alive has made a world of difference to me. They have given me my flowers while I'm living instead of when I'm dead. For this, I am eternally grateful. Tasha was always there and really stepped up to the plate to become one of my best friends and protectors. Another blessing came in the form of the ability to write this book that I hope will be able to help other men and women through this kind of crazy.

The title *Shadow Dancing* came to mind because with a *shadow* you only see the outline of a person and never can see who they really are. And *dancing* because when you are not being who you are, you are always dancing around how you should be.

It is my prayer that the world can learn to let people be who they are without fear of being harmed or made to feel less than human by those who say they believe in God. Let the world begin to treat gays and lesbians the way Jesus would, with love! Hopefully, the day will come when women on the "down low" can take off that mask of deception and be who and what they really are and stop shadow dancing.